BLOOMING
THROUGH THE CRACKS:
Inspiring Stories of Resilience

Sandra Damiani

CONTENTS

To all the people who offer their hand
to anyone who is struggling,

Thank you.

This book is for you.
You are the champion of change in the world!

SHATTERED BOUNDARIES

The air crackled with anticipation as the senior class stood shoulder-to-shoulder on the sun-drenched sidewalk. The vibrant colors of their caps and gowns stood out against the stark brick facade of the school. Voices rose and fell in animated conversation about late-night study sessions, shared dreams, and inside jokes.

Ms. Johnson, the twelfth-grade science teacher, emerged from the school's side entrance. She walked toward the students, but they were so engrossed in their shared memories and excitement that they didn't notice her approaching.

Ms. Johnson cleared her throat. "Students," she said.

The students turned to look at her.

"I need to remind you of the rules," Ms. Johnson said. "First, please maintain your composure until the last person has received their diploma."

Ms. Johnson paused to make sure that the students were listening.

Then, after she went over a few more rules, she said, "Please walk slowly into the auditorium and take your seats."

As the graduates entered the hall, the hushed whispers gave way to a thunderous eruption of applause. Gerald and Jolene walked with their heads held high, a mix of emotions playing across their faces – relief, accomplishment, and a touch of bittersweet anticipation for the future.

Inspirational student speeches started the ceremony. Their names were called as they walked across the stage. The principal was the final speaker at the podium. He congratulated everyone and told them that they were free to go.

Out of everything said that day, the word *free* meant the most to Gerald. Finally, he was free to leave his parents' house. Gerald hated it when he had to listen to the jarring thud of his father's fists hitting his mother. He'd bury himself under the scratchy covers in his bed, pulling them up over his head, and then he would squeeze his eyes shut, willing himself to fall asleep, but the choked sobs that escaped his mother's lips were like icy fingers crawling down his spine.

Jolene couldn't wait to get out of her parents' house either. She had called her stepmother *Mom* since she was three years old but had never found it in her heart to like her. Her mother died when she was young, and her father remarried shortly after that. Jolene's dad and stepmother had two children together, Joey and Mary.

One afternoon, when Jolene was eight years old, she was watching cartoons in the living room when she spotted Mary's doll on the coffee table. Jolene was attracted to the doll's long, flowing hair and big blue eyes, so she picked the doll up and pretended to feed her some cake.

As Jolene's stepmother walked past the living room, she noticed Jolene playing with Mary's doll.

"Jolene, what are you doing with Mary's doll?" she asked.

Jolene froze. She knew she was in trouble. "I was just holding it," she said.

Jolene's stepmother walked over to where Jolene was playing and snatched the doll out of her hand. After tucking the doll under her arm, she warned Jolene to ask permission before she touched Joey's or Mary's toys.

Jolene was confused. She didn't understand why her stepmother was so quick to punish her for playing with Mary's doll when Joey had come into her bedroom and broken her tea set the day before, but he didn't get in trouble.

Jolene would ask her stepmother, "Why do you treat them like they are so special?'

Her stepmother's reaction was: "Don't you dare question me. Do as you are told, or you'll regret it."

Jolene would ask her father: "Why does Mom let them get away with everything?"

Her father would answer: "You need to listen to your mother. You are the oldest, so of course, more is expected of you."

Gerald and Jolene started dating in the tenth grade. They could talk to each other about anything and knew how much the other one wanted to escape their bad situations at home. In the twelfth grade, they decided to get married after they graduated and swore to be nothing like their parents.

One year after Gerald and Jolene were married, they had their first child. It was a boy, and they named him Nathan. Gerald and Jolene were determined to be better parents to Nathan than their parents had been to them. A year later, Nathan had a sister. Two years after that, Nathan had a brother.

Gerald and Jolene were twenty-two years old and had three young children. Gerald worked as an appliance salesman, and Jolene was a stay-at-home mom. Jolene was exhausted from caring for the children all day and night, and Gerald was feeling the strain of making ends meet.

Gerald's appliance store shared a video on social media showcasing a dishwasher's ability to clean a pan half-filled with lasagna. After the video went viral, customers flocked to the store to learn more about the dishwasher's specifications and features.

One housewife came into the store three times to inquire about the dishwasher. She kept asking Gerald to reassure her that the video was accurate.

Was the pan in the commercial nonstick?

Was the dishwasher soap used in the video different from what she could buy in the store?

When the customer showed up for the third day in a row, Gerald decided she was wasting his time. She was spending too much time over-thinking a dishwasher to ever buy it.

So when she asked if the dishwasher would clean a pan if she burned the lasagna, Gerald asked the customer if she routinely burned things she cooked. His remark made the customer so upset that she started crying. When Gerald's boss saw the customer crying, he fired Gerald on the spot. Gerald grabbed his keys and stormed out of the store.

As Gerald parked the car in the driveway, the crunch of gravel under the tires echoed in the still air. Hearing the familiar sound, Jolene came out the front door just as Gerald stepped out of the car.

Jolene walked towards Gerald, saying, "I need you to get some more diapers. I only have one left."

Gerald walked past Jolene, ignoring her, and went inside the house.

Jolene followed him. "Did you hear me?"

Gerald continued to ignore her.

Jolene yelled. "Are you deaf?"

Suddenly, a loud crack echoed as Jolene's neck jerked to the side. She was knocked off balance and scrambled to stand up straight. The crisp sting of pain was overshadowed by the sudden and shocking realization that Gerald had just crossed a line she never thought he would. Gerald had slapped her across the face.

Gerald felt a wave of guilt wash over him as he looked at Jolene, her eyes filled with tears. He had always promised himself that he would never be like his father, that he would never hit his wife.

"I'm so sorry," Gerald said. "I don't know what came over me."

Gerald's slap shattered Jolene's self-esteem, self-respect, and dig-nity— everything that made her feel good about herself. Jolene was torn between two choices: to swallow her pride and forgive her husband, keeping the picture of a happy family intact, or let her anger show and risk worsening the situation or losing her marriage. In the end, she chose to forgive Gerald but worried that he might repeat his abusive behavior in the future.

Later that night, Gerald told Jolene he had been fired from the appliance store. Jolene was surprised that he didn't seem the least bit upset. Instead, he was relieved about not having to listen to customers complaining.

When Gerald woke up the next day, he was determined to find a new job. He spent the morning searching the computer for job openings that matched his skills and experience. After a few days of searching, he began receiving calls from companies interested in hiring him.

Gerald's enthusiasm and excitement each time he went for a job interview caused Jolene to reflect on how boring her life had become. She loved her children but was tired of being cooped up in the house all day. Jolene decided that she wanted to go to work.

Jolene worked as a cashier in a local department store during high school. With her previous experience, she decided to apply for a retail job. After she got hired, Jolene couldn't believe how much of her hard-earned money was going towards daycare.

Once all the children were in school, Jolene relied on Nathan to walk his siblings to and from school and take care of them while she was at work. After Nathan took on the responsibility of looking after his younger siblings, Gerald and Jolene were finally able to start saving money for a down payment on a house. They worked hard and saved money for two years, and finally, they were able to buy a fixer-upper in the suburbs.

After three months of owning their new home, the initial excitement faded as reality set in. When they received a five-figure estimate for a cracked heat exchanger, Gerald panicked due to their already tight budget, and Jolene felt like their dream home had turned into a financial nightmare. To cover the cost, Gerald got a second job, but the leaky roof, a sudden gurgle in the kitchen sink, and their children's worn-out shoes remained a threat to their financial security.

Jolene and Gerald's money fights, a familiar dance of blame and despair, became a nightly ritual. Jolene would accuse Gerald of reckless spending on his hobbies and not understanding the weight of responsibility. Gerald resented Jolene for blaming him for their mess and for her lack of appreciation for the number of hours he worked.

When his parents started arguing, Nathan would hide in his bedroom. When his mother's voice became a high-pitched screech and his father's retorts turned into guttural roars, it was only a matter of time before things became violent.

After the fights ended and everything was quiet, Jolene would often come into Nathan's bedroom. He patiently listened to his mom while his siblings were out with their friends or upstairs in their room playing video games. She'd tell him how much she hated Gerald and how he had promised to be different from his father but was exactly like him. Sometimes, it felt like his mom told him the same horror stories about his father repeatedly. But he never pointed this out because he felt obligated to react like it was all new.

Before Jolene would leave Nathan's room, she would tell him, "I can always count on my little man to be there for me."

Jolene's dependence on Nathan to take care of his siblings and to listen to her complain about his father caused her to focus a lot of attention on him. Nathan's extra attention from his mom caused a lot of rivalry between him and his siblings. Anytime Nathan got into a fight with his brother or sister, they would accuse him of being their mother's favorite.

Nathan didn't feel like the favorite. He was just trying to support his mom. It made him sad—his siblings had each other; he had no one.

Everything changed the year Nathan graduated from high school. His parents were in the kitchen, arguing about green peas. Gerald preferred corn with pork chops, but Jolene had forgotten to buy corn on her way home from work, so she decided to serve green peas for dinner that night instead.

As Nathan walked in the back door, he heard Gerald accusing Jolene of not keeping her side of the bargain. She was responsible for planning the meals, and he was responsible for earning most of the money in the house. Gerald was about to hit Jolene just as Nathan walked into the kitchen.

Nathan jumped in between his parents. "You are not going to hit her anymore."

Nathan's father reacted by trying to hit him. Nathan grabbed his hand and said, "That's enough."

Nathan's father smirked at him. "So you think you're a big man. Are you going to hit me?"

Nathan wasn't afraid of his father anymore. He just resented him for the way he treated his mother. Nathan knew why his father got away with how he treated his mother. It was because size does matter in a fight. His father was twice the size of his mother.

Nathan let go of his father's hand and slowly said, "You will never hit Mom again."

Nathan's father laughed out loud and turned around to walk out the door. As he was leaving, he said, "You were always your mother's favorite."

Shortly after Nathan confronted his father in the kitchen, his parents began leading separate lives. His dad relocated to the spare bedroom in the basement and would often disappear for entire weekends. His mom would return home late on Saturday nights, well after midnight.

Watching the family disintegrate, Nathan promised himself that things would be different when he had a family of his own. He wasn't going to be the kind of man who cycles through hitting his wife, then quickly apologizing to get things back to normal.

Exactly how much his life had changed became clear to Nathan one night when he was on a date. As Nathan and his girlfriend walked into the restaurant, he noticed his mom with some friends at the bar. He watched as Jolene picked up a glass of whiskey, swung her head back, and poured the shot into her mouth.

As Jolene set the glass back on the bar, she noticed Nathan. She walked over to where Nathan and his girlfriend were standing and invited them to come over to the bar and meet her friends.

Nathan quickly made an excuse. He and his date planned on eating a quick bite and then heading to the movie theater because the movie they were seeing was starting soon.

Nathan had never had an idealized view of his family, but now he was confused about who was causing his family to be so broken. His mom, who had never been much of a drinker, was starting to drink more and more. His father was rarely at home, but he was always so angry when he did come home.

Later that year, Nathan enrolled in an out-of-state college to get as far away from all the confusion in his family as possible. Initially, he came home for a few holiday breaks but quickly stopped. He didn't see the point when he was spending all his time alone in the house. His mom and siblings were always out doing their own thing. His dad occasionally stopped by the house, but he didn't seem to live there anymore.

After graduation, Nathan eagerly stepped into the bustling world of marketing. He took his instinctual sense of responsibility developed by supporting and protecting his mother and poured it into his career. He refused to ever again feel like a failure, like the times when he had to listen to his father hitting his mother. His resolve left him with an enormous amount of pressure to succeed.

Nathan's hard work and commitment to his job earned him the opportunity to oversee one of the company's largest clients. However, when his female colleague started feeling jealous about not getting the same recognition as Nathan, she asked Nathan in a condescending tone if he ever planned on taking a vacation. Nathan interpreted her approach as an attempt to undermine his capabilities and make him feel like a helpless child.

"I don't need anyone to mother me," Nathan proclaimed. "I work ten-hour days, six days a week, because my success is what I expect of myself. So don't treat me like I'm your child."

Nathan had a high-paying job and a corner office, but he was stressed out and questioned if there was more to life than work. Nathan was apprehensive about taking a step back from his work, fearing he would lose his status as a top performer. However, he was also aware that he would eventually burn out if he didn't make a change.

Nathan worked in a building that had a restaurant on the second floor. This restaurant was popular among the lunch crowd and had several tables and a long counter. People who came to the restaurant alone often chose to sit at the counter. It was amusing to watch the short-order cook flip burgers and the servers fill up two glasses of soda at a time, especially for someone who had no one to talk to.

Nathan and Molly, a colleague who worked in a different office, sat next to each other at the lunch counter one day and struck up a conversation. Nathan and Molly discovered that they both shared an interest in reading and soon found themselves discussing the books they had read. As they talked, they learned a lot about each other and found themselves revealing things about their lives they never thought they'd tell anyone.

Nathan thought Molly was attractive, but as the lunch hour passed, he became more distracted about returning to work. Molly liked how she felt when she made eye contact with Nathan and hoped he might ask her out.

The next day, and the day after, Molly and Nathan would seek each other out as they came into the restaurant for lunch. They came to see their time together as the highlight of their day.

Molly and Nathan were sitting at the counter eating lunch one day when a couple came into the restaurant with their young daughter. Nathan and Molly overheard the little girl asking her mother if they could eat at the counter. The mother told her daughter there weren't enough empty seats for them. There were only two empty seats together, and they needed three. Molly smiled at the little girl and got up. She said she would move over to the stool on the other side of her friend Nathan. That way, the family could eat at the counter together. The little girl returned Molly's smile and said thank you.

Nathan found it relaxing to watch as Molly picked up her soda and moved to make room for the little girl and her family to sit down. Nathan thought that one day, Molly would make a great mom. He started imagining what she would look like when she was pregnant and knew he wanted to be the father of her children.

Nathan asked Molly to go on a date that night, and a year later, he proposed to her. After getting married, they started a family and bought a brownstone in the city.

One night, Molly noticed a small puddle of water on the floor in the living room. She followed the trail of water back to the radiator, which was dripping water from a small hole in the side. She quickly placed a pot under the drip to catch the water and prevent it from spreading. However, when the drip turned into a steady stream, Molly became concerned that the pipe might burst, which could cause hot water to spray all over the house.

Nathan was working late, so Molly gave him a call.

Nathan was perturbed. "You need to learn to handle things on your own."

Molly said, "I would have taken care of it if I knew where the turn-off switch was in the basement. But bringing the baby down there didn't seem safe when I didn't know what I was doing."

Nathan knew something more profound than a switch in the basement was coming between him and his wife. When Molly called him, it triggered memories of his mother's demanding behavior while he was growing up. Nathan had always been his mother's "little man," the person she came to when she fought with his father or needed help with his younger siblings.

Now, Nathan was scrutinizing and pressuring Molly because he didn't want Molly to bring him all her problems like his mother did when he was growing up. After thinking it through, Nathan remembered that Molly was her own person with her own unique needs and desires. He was wrong to project his fears onto his wife or assume she would behave the same way his mother did.

A week later, Nathan's mother called to say she would be coming for the weekend. Nathan knew his mother could be demanding and difficult to deal with, but he still felt a sense of obligation towards her. Instead of voicing his concerns about his mother, he decided to buy her favorite cookies from the store to make her feel welcome.

Jolene had news to share when she got there.

"I told your father I want a divorce, and he has agreed."

Nathan immediately realized his mother expected him to support her in her decision.

So, instead of talking to her about his feelings, he said, "I want you to be happy."

Jolene replied, "I'm going to get the life I deserve, finally."

Jolene started calling Nathan every day after the divorce was final. She wanted to keep Nathan updated about how things were going with her newfound freedom.

One night, Jolene called Nathan around midnight. Just a month ago, her life had been filled with stolen kisses, whispered promises, and laughter that echoed through her apartment. Then, a phone call from her boyfriend caused her world to come crashing down. His voice was cold and distant; the words "it's over" left Jolene questioning what went wrong.

"I always got a lot of attention from guys in high school," Jolene boasted. "He was lucky that I went out with him."

Nathan didn't say anything. He only listened, just like always.

The following day, Molly confronted Nathan about all the attention he was giving his mother.

"Your mom calls you every day, and you always take her call. Last night, she woke up the baby. Two days ago, you left the dinner table when she called. I could understand if it were an emergency, but why doesn't she think about what we might be doing before she calls?"

Nathan explained, "I have to take her calls. I would feel guilty if she needed me to fix something for her and I wasn't there."

"Why doesn't she call you in the afternoon when it's a slow period at your job?"

"She watches her soaps in the afternoon. She doesn't like anyone to call her between one and three o'clock in the afternoon."

Molly was furious. "You need to stop worrying about making her upset. What is the worst thing that will happen? The world won't stop spinning if she gets upset. What about making me upset? I need to be your priority."

"You don't understand. When I was a kid, my mom felt like I was the only one who could help her. She calls me now because she still depends on me to be there for her," Nathan said.

Molly took a deep breath. She knew that she was treading on dangerous ground. Nathan loved his mom and had never spoken about any of her faults.

Molly hesitantly said, "I understand that your mom is an adult. You are not her husband. You are her son. You get to decide how big of a part she plays in your life."

Nathan leaned in close as Molly spoke, his eyes never leaving her face.

Molly continued, "I don't want this thing that you have with your mom to affect how I react to her. I love your mom too, but you cannot save her anymore. You are first to me, and I need to know I am first to you. You need to show me some love."

Pulling Molly close, Nathan said, "You have been a part of everything good in my life. I'm going to talk to my mom."

Before Nathan had time to talk with Jolene, she showed up unannounced for a weekend visit with her new boyfriend. Nathan and Molly weren't prepared for guests, so they went to a local restaurant for dinner.

Once they got to the restaurant, Jolene and her boyfriend started ordering drinks. Nathan and Molly joined them for a drink before dinner but didn't keep pace with them after that. Jolene and her boyfriend drank three more drinks with their meal.

After returning home from the restaurant, Jolene retrieved a bottle of wine from her car. Although the wine was intended to be a gift for Nathan and Molly, Jolene couldn't resist indulging in it herself. Nathan got a corkscrew from the kitchen drawer, and Jolene opened the bottle.

Nathan listened to his mom slurring her words. Her boyfriend didn't seem to notice; he was intoxicated, too. They told a story about going to a show downtown and getting a hotel so they didn't have to drive home.

Getting a hotel was Nathan's cue. Encouraging his mom and boyfriend to sleep it off, he told them that Molly had set up the guest room for them. When Nathan noticed that his mom was struggling to follow the conversation, he dug his fingers into his neck muscles, trying to massage away the tension.

Nathan sighed, "It's been a long day. I need to get some rest."

As Nathan lay in bed and stared at the ceiling, he thought how seeing his mother so incoherent, so altered by the alcohol, made him feel a strange mix of protectiveness and aversion. He couldn't reconcile this unfamiliar version of his mom with the woman he knew and loved.

Nathan had a revelation as the clock on the bedside table taunted him with its glowing red numbers: 3:02 AM. He knew he could not be the man to take care of his mom, even if she never had the man she needed.

Finally, around five o'clock, a weary resignation settled over him. Nathan knew the battle against sleep was lost. Instead of fighting, he pushed himself up, the worn mattress groaning beneath him.

Nathan heard the familiar rhythmic hiss of the coffee maker as he walked toward the kitchen. Jolene was sitting at the table, holding her coffee mug and looking down. Nathan poured himself a cup of coffee and slid into the chair opposite his mother.

Nathan asked, "How are you doing?"

"I've got a small hangover."

"Ever since I was a boy, I've worried about your being okay."

"I know, you've always been there for me," Jolene said.

"All those years when I was growing up, there was always so much chaos in the house."

Jolene interrupted, "I know all about chaos. My stepmother was horrible to me. I always wanted things to be different for you."

Nathan cleared his throat: "What I'm trying to tell you is that I need my mom. I want you to be happy, but sometimes, it's hard for me to handle dealing with all your relationships."

"Where is all this coming from?" Jolene asked.

"I have responsibilities to my own family now," Nathan said. "I want to be the man in Molly's life, the father in my child's life, but not the person you depend on to listen to all your problems."

Jolene was too stunned to speak. She stared at Nathan, unable to believe she had thought relying on him to be her support system was okay.

Finally, Jolene said, "I've leaned on you too much. I'm sorry about that."

Jolene got up and came over to where Nathan was sitting. She kissed him on the top of his head and told him she needed to go upstairs and get dressed.

When Jolene came down, she told Nathan she and her boyfriend needed to get going.

"I'll call soon to find a good time to visit my grandbaby."

Nathan felt guilty. "I really need you to be okay."

Jolene looked at him and smiled.

"You never have to worry about me being okay again. I have such a strong son. We are both going to be just fine."

Nathan hugged his mom. For the first time in his life, he believed that the only thing that his mom wanted from him was for him to be happy. Finally, an unspeakable burden had been lifted from his shoulders. He was free to be his mother's son.

THICK-SKINNED

As Chrystal set the plate of crackers and cheese on Nick's desk, she smiled. Nick would be home any minute now, and he was always hungry after spending all day at school.

Chrystal turned and walked into the bathroom, closing the door behind her. She turned on the shower and stepped inside, letting the water melt away the tension in her muscles as it ran over her skin.

The hot water would run out soon, so she reached into the shower caddy for the shampoo. She squirted a quarter-sized amount into her hand. As she worked it through her hair, it began to lather.

Chrystal had been in the bathroom for a few minutes, trying to relax and take a break from the chaos of the day, when suddenly she froze, listening.

She turned off the shower. Yelling was coming from outside the bathroom door. It sounded like a child, and they were definitely upset.

Chrystal jumped out of the shower with bubbles in her hair. She wrapped herself in a towel and stepped into the hallway.

The yelling was coming from her son's room. Chrystal rushed down the hall to Nick's room. Opening the door quickly, Chrystal stepped inside. Nick was sitting at his desk, staring intently at the calculator in his hand. His lips moved as he punched in another number.

Chrystal asked Nick if he was hurt, but he ignored her and continued to work on his math homework like nothing was wrong. Chrystal noticed the crackers and cheese she had left for a snack were in the trash can beside Nick's desk. She asked him again if he was hurt. When he didn't answer, she asked him why his snack was in the trash can.

Nick angrily looked up from his math book. "You know that I like grapes better than crackers and cheese. There are grapes in the fridge. I don't know why you didn't get them for me."

Chrystal didn't say anything as she hurried out of Nick's room. She went into her bedroom and grabbed her robe before going downstairs.

Chrystal turned on the light in the kitchen and took a cluster of grapes out of the refrigerator. She grabbed a plate from the cupboard and a napkin from the holder. She put the napkin on the plate and rinsed the grapes off. Then, she set the grapes on top of the napkin. Nick liked the napkin under the grapes so the plate wouldn't be full of water.

Nick thanked Chrystal when she brought the grapes into his bedroom. His politeness was an expected part of the exchange after he got what he wanted from his mother.

The shampoo was still in Chrystal's hair, so she returned to the shower. As the shampoo bubbles rinsed down the drain, Chrystal envisioned Nick standing at the chalkboard in his math class, working on a complex math problem. His teacher was standing beside him, smiling at his brilliance.

Nick's father and his teachers accused Chrystal of over-indulging Nick on many different occasions, but Chrystal would just laugh to herself when anyone told her that she was blind to the ways her son acted. She knew that Nick was capable of great things, and she was going to do everything she could to help him reach his full potential.

Nick believed that the world owed him everything because of the way his mother spoiled him, but the one place where he earned his recognition was on the basketball court. His hard work and talent earned him a spot on the varsity basketball team in ninth grade. He was promoted to the team's point guard position in the tenth grade and held that position until he graduated.

The final basketball game of the season in Nick's senior year was against the school's number-one rival. Nick's school had played against this team on their home turf earlier in the season and had barely beaten them by three points. Even though the final game was on the rival's home court, Nick was determined to win again.

During the bus ride to the game, Nick started snatching the basketball from the other players when they tried to pass it between the seats. Nick's behavior quickly destroyed the team's playful camaraderie and caused resentment at the coach for not intervening and stopping the chaos.

Once the bus pulled into the school parking lot, the team's eyes lit up with renewed determination. They exchanged fist bumps and encouraging grins, the air buzzing with a sudden surge of energy.

The chatter and laughter of Nick's teammates were irrelevant and muted compared to the roar in his head, the strategizing, the anticipation, the burning need to prove himself. His jaw clenched, teeth grinding subtly against each other.

The game was close from the start. Nick's team jumped to an early lead, but the rival team quickly fought back. They traded baskets for most of the first half, and the score was tied at halftime.

The second half was even more intense. Both teams played their hearts out, and the lead changed hands several times.

With forty seconds left in the game, the score was tied. The parents from the two schools were on their feet, cheering as the two teams battled for the win.

Nick caught the pass and started advancing down the court. He knew that the defenders were coming up behind him, so he had to make a decision quickly.

Nick saw an open forward and attempted to pass. A guard on the other team intercepted the play. The guard moved the ball down the court and quickly took a shot. The ball swished through the net, and the rival team won the game by one point.

Nick's unsportsmanlike conduct was on full display when he refused to shake hands with the opposing team after losing the game. The disapproving murmurs in the handshake line caused Nick to storm off the court.

As Nick entered the locker room, he slammed the door shut and sat down on the bench. Clenching his fists and staring at the wall, Nick could feel his heart racing. Suddenly, he let out a guttural roar and punched the hard metal bench, causing a loud clang to echo through the silent locker room.

The players entered the locker room one by one and walked past Nick to their lockers. As soon as the last lock clicked shut, a silence took over the room. Suddenly, the locker room door opened and the coach entered the room.

"Alright, team," the coach announced loudly. "The bus is loading in five minutes, so pack your bags and meet me outside."

Nick didn't want to ride back with his teammates, who he believed had cost him the game, so he got permission from the coach to ride back in the car with his father.

At the start of the drive home, Nick had nothing to say. His father was relieved by the silence, but he could hear Nick grinding his teeth, a clear indication that he had something on his mind.

Nick looked out the car window as he replayed the moment his team lost the game in his mind. The memory caused him to clench his fist so tightly that his nails bit into his palm. Unable to control the tremor in his hand, Nick slammed his fist against the dashboard.

"The forward was an idiot," Nick proclaimed. "He should have noticed when the guard ran in front of him. If he had been paying attention, he would have caught the ball. It isn't my fault the team is a bunch of morons."

Nick's father knew Nick didn't like to be scrutinized and was sensitive to criticism, so he opted to make him feel good about his choices. He knew that was what Nick's mother would expect him to do; she had insisted it was the way to build his son's self-confidence. Nick's father wasn't sure, but he'd never had much self-confidence.

He said, "Look, Nick. The forward saw you moving the ball down the court. If he had gotten in the right position, then he could have caught the ball and made the shot. Your team would have won the game."

When Nick returned to school, he stopped wearing his varsity basketball jacket. He refused to be associated with a bunch of losers.

Nick moved on to the last big event for his senior year in high school: the prom. Looking good at the biggest dance party of the year was important to Nick, so he started perfecting his moves in front of the mirror at home. *Everyone will be watching me*, Nick thought. *Wishing they could dance like me when they step onto the dance floor.*

Excited about finding a date who could make him look good and impress others, Nick started thinking about asking JoAnn to be his date for the prom. He had seen her dance at other school parties and knew that she would be the best dancer beside himself at the prom. JoAnn's boyfriend, Jerry, was the only obstacle standing in Nick's way.

Every day at precisely 11:45, Jerry and JoAnn would rush through the library to claim their usual table in the courtyard. Countless lunches had worn the paint on the table, but their preferred spot gave them a clear view of who would play the winning playlist's first notes.

In the courtyard, there was an unspoken rule that whoever arrived first had the privilege of playing their playlist for everyone to listen to that day. However, if they didn't want to choose the music, they could hand it over to the next person who arrived. This was the rule, but in reality, only a select few with cutting-edge playlists took turns playing their songs on their phones. If someone's favorite tune came on, they might even entertain everyone by dancing around the courtyard.

One week before the prom, Nick strutted over to the table where Jerry and Joann were eating lunch together in the courtyard.

In a loud voice, Nick dared Jerry. "So I know that you must have some cool dance moves. I mean, going to the prom with JoAnn and all. Why don't you show us what you've got?"

Jerry winced. He didn't care about dancing. He left that to JoAnn. He was more interested in football.

"Nick," Jerry said, his voice firm despite the rising panic in his stomach, "Why don't you get lost?"

Nick's face contorted. "Come on, don't be a scaredy-cat! One little song, that's all I ask!" His voice, already loud, climbed another octave, drawing unwanted attention from nearby students.

Stung, Jerry conceded. He stood up and miserably tried to dance. Everyone eating lunch in the courtyard laughed as he awkwardly began flinging his arms about without moving any other part of his body. Feeling like a fool, Jerry stormed off.

The following day, Nick approached Jerry to clarify that he had only talked to him in the courtyard because he was interested in dancing, and he never expected Jerry to get up and dance. Nick blamed the whole incident on a misunderstanding and then offered to teach Jerry some of his dance moves as a way to put the matter behind them.

Jerry was hesitant at first, but once Nick convinced Jerry that he had misinterpreted the situation, Nick added, "I'll need about a month to get you up to speed."

Jerry looked at Nick, confused. The prom was less than a week away.

Nick continued, "I know you don't want to embarrass JoAnn at the prom. She is a sweet girl and deserves to have a good time."

Jerry had the feeling Nick was waiting for him to say something, but he didn't know what to say.

Nick continued, "Imagine if you were in an important game—THE important game— and one player on your team was really weak. It could ruin everything."

Jerry had never thought about the prom in that way.

"I can do you a favor. I'll take JoAnn to the prom. I like to dance, and we both know that dancing is important to JoAnn."

Nick's offer felt like a ticking time bomb, but it mattered more to Jerry that JoAnn had a good time at the prom than whether he went himself.

The next day after school, Jerry found JoAnn and admitted feeling awkward about dancing. He explained that he cared about her and that Nick had offered to take her to the prom strictly as a friend. JoAnn didn't want Jerry to do something he was uncomfortable with, so she agreed to go with Nick.

Nick arrived on time at JoAnn's house with a beautiful corsage. He looked dashing in his black tuxedo, and JoAnn was equally captivating in her long green gown.

Stepping onto the dance floor, Nick attempted to take the lead. However, JoAnn misunderstood his intentions and thought he was trying to engage in a friendly competition. JoAnn continued dancing her way and enjoying her evening with her girlfriends. Nick added even more daring dance moves and bragged to anyone who would listen about how easy it was for him to get a hot date for the prom. No one was impressed, but Nick was oblivious to their lack of enthusiasm.

Driving home after the prom, Nick asked JoAnn, "Wasn't my move on the last dance amazing? So many people loved it."

Growing tired of Nick's constant need to be the center of attention, JoAnn rolled her eyes before playing along, "Sure, you can dance."

Feeling like JoAnn understood him on a profound level, Nick asked JoAnn, "Why don't we go to the lake with the other seniors? They are going to watch the sunrise in the morning."

"I better not. I would if Jerry was here. You know what I mean.'"

"I don't understand. You wanted to come to the prom with me," Nick said.

"That was because Jerry told me we were going as friends."

"Believe what you want," Nick smirked.

JoAnn insisted, "Take me home right now."

Friends entered and exited Nick's life very quickly in high school. People would remain his friend until they realized how skilled Nick was at making up stories and getting his way.

At the graduation ceremony, several classmates accused Nick of only being concerned about himself at his friends' expense. Nick's reaction was that he was glad graduation was here. He was finally getting away from all the jealous losers in high school.

Nick started college in the fall and quickly noticed how the guys wearing Greek letters on their shirts enjoyed a certain status among the other students. Nick wanted to join this exclusive group, so he started attending the fraternity rush events.

During a fraternity rush event, Nick shared a story about how his high school friendships had a powerful impact on his life. He talked about how he changed his plans for an after-prom party to support his friend. Nick also mentioned that he had led his high school basketball team to victory. When he expressed his desire to contribute similar skills and passion to the fraternity, Nick was invited to join.

At one of the Friday night parties, a fellow brother approached Nick. He wanted Nick to help him move out of the dorms and into an apartment off campus.

"I have better things to do than move furniture," Nick said.

His fraternity brother looked at him, confused. "I don't understand how you can be a member of this fraternity and not help out your brother."

Nick got the impression that his fraternity brother was attacking him. "If you were smarter, this wouldn't be a problem for you."

Nick patted him on the back, then yelled, "Get a diaper. Someone just messed all over themselves."

After graduating from college, Nick embarked on his professional career. Shortly after Nick started working, he overheard Stewart, a guy in the office next door, outlining his plan to save the company a lot of money. Nick immediately knew this was his idea. It was there, fully formed, in his mind; Stewart's words had just nudged it loose. He doubted that Stewart even knew what he was saying.

Nick quickly sent out an email detailing his idea to his boss. His boss was impressed. He called a meeting to go over Nick's idea in two days.

When Stewart heard that his original idea was the subject of an upcoming meeting, he approached Nick about co-chairing the presentation. Nick agreed.

Nick took the lead in the meeting. He gave an overview of his timeline and then passed the outsourcing requirements to his co-chair. Stewart was surprised to be asked to present about outsourcing. He didn't know much about the financial or supply side. The technical side was his forte.

Stewart attempted to wing his presentation without appearing incompetent to the boss. But after it became abundantly clear that he knew nothing about negotiating contracts with vendors, Nick stepped back into his role as the lead chair. He provided all the names of outsourcing companies and associated costs.

After the meeting concluded and everyone was back in the office, Stewart wanted to discuss his shared lead on the project. He was angry at Nick for stealing his idea and trying to humiliate him in front of their boss.

Nick quickly pointed out to Stewart that it wasn't his fault he had embarrassed himself by not knowing about outsourcing. But after seeing how Stewart wasn't familiar with all the latest business practices, it would be best for the company's sake for Nick to take the lead.

Nick immediately went to his computer and emailed his boss, cc'ing Stewart. In the email, he identified himself as the point person for any questions as the project moved forward.

Even though Nick stole his co-worker's plan to save the company money, Nick still managed to be the one to receive all the credit and glowing reviews from the managers. But when Nick got passed over for a promotion, he started to wonder what was holding him back.

One day, Nick talked to his friend, Sarah, about his situation. Sarah was a human resources manager at another company and had a lot of experience with promotions. She told Nick that she had seen cases where single people were passed over for promotions because their employers assumed they would be less committed to their work.

Based on Sarah's information, Nick immediately asked Denise, a secretary in one of the offices down the hall, to date him. Nick believed Denise was pretty enough to cause the other guys to envy him but not so formidable that he couldn't exert his influence over her.

On their fourth date, Denise and Nick decided to try a local restaurant known for its spicy salsa. After the hostess took them to their table, their waitress came with some salsa and chips and took their drink order.

After a few minutes, the waitress came back with their drinks and asked if they were ready to order. Denise decided to go with the taco salad, while Nick asked the waitress for suggestions. She recommended the burrito platter, which was among the most popular dishes on the menu.

Nick appreciated the waitress's attentive behavior and ordered what she had suggested.

After finishing their meal, Nick left the table to use the restroom. After fifteen minutes had passed, Denise became worried and decided to check up on him. As Denise walked towards the restroom, she spotted Nick standing by the kitchen entrance, smiling and chatting with their waitress.

Denise walked towards Nick and their waitress. When they saw her approaching, they stopped talking and turned around to look at her.

Denise's voice was filled with anxiety as she exclaimed, "I got worried when you were gone for so long."

Nick replied, "You found me, so let's go!"

Nick approached Denise and forcibly grabbed her arm. He held her arm tightly and pulled her towards the cash register to pay for their meal. Nick didn't speak to Denise during the transaction, hoping to make her feel guilty for interrupting his conversation with the waitress.

As they left the restaurant, Denise said, "I couldn't help but notice; it seemed like you were flirting with the waitress."

Nick answered abruptly, "I can't help it if women want to throw themselves at me. If you weren't so insecure, this wouldn't bother you."

Denise and Nick had been talking about the movie they planned to watch at Denise's house over dinner, but the ride back to her house was replaced by a heavy silence that spoke louder than any words could. Once they pulled into the driveway, Denise told Nick she didn't feel good. They would have to watch the movie another night, but she would call him later.

Nick tried texting and calling Denise for the next two days without any response. When he could finally catch up with her at work, he asked her, "What's going on? You haven't been answering my texts or phone calls."

Denise answered in a matter-of-fact tone, "This doesn't work for me. Don't call or text me anymore."

A smug grin appeared on Nick's face as he said, "Sure, whatever."

Looking for a partner who could fulfill his needs, Nick noticed Chloe, a woman who went to his gym. Despite never having had a conversation with her beyond a casual hello, he decided to ask her out for dinner and a movie.

Chloe was excited about her first date with Nick and wanted to look her best. She searched her closet for the perfect outfit, but couldn't find anything suitable. After days of searching, Chloe finally stumbled upon a blue dress that had been tucked away in a forgotten corner. The dress was made of a soft and comfortable fabric, and it had a flattering fit that made Chloe feel confident and beautiful.

On their date night, Nick wanted to find out how valuable a partner Chloe would be, so as they walked into the restaurant, Nick smiled at Chloe and said, "You look pretty tonight. Your dress is nice, but the color doesn't complement your skin tone."

All the effort Chloe had poured into selecting the perfect outfit, the hours spent searching her closet, the careful consideration of every detail— it all felt suddenly meaningless in the face of Nick's casual dismissal.

While trying to decide if Nick was trying to make her feel self-conscious, Chloe remembered that he said she was pretty. Chloe thought, *Maybe he didn't understand how offensive his comment about the color of my dress had been.*

Taking a deep breath, she lifted her chin. The blue dress might not have been Nick's preference, but it was hers. Rather than letting Nick's comment cause an argument, Chloe decided to move on.

"That's interesting. What one person might find flattering, another person might not."

Nick looked at Chloe and smiled. Her response proved that she wasn't wasting his time like Denise had. Chloe hadn't challenged what he said. She was willing to go with the flow and not make a big deal over everything.

Over the next few months, Chloe's heart would race whenever she heard Nick's voice. Each syllable held a whispered promise; every word was a caress that sent goosebumps rippling across her skin. Their secret language caused the world to shimmer with an intensity Chloe had never noticed before.

When Nick made reservations for Saturday night at a mountain resort, Chloe couldn't help but smile at the thought of cozying up by the fireplace. She started planning her outfits and packing her bags, eager to spend a romantic night with Nick.

On the morning of their trip, Nick's car sped down the highway without the weekly bumper-to-bumper traffic, letting them pull into the parking lot at the resort two hours ahead of their reservation time. As they walked toward the hotel, Nick's hand in hers, Chloe's pulse quickened, balanced between the comfort of Nick's presence and the anticipation of the night to come.

The lobby's air was heavy, burdened by the collective sigh of travelers waiting to check into their room. After what felt like an eternity spent inching forward in the line, Chloe and Nick reached the front. When the clerk at the desk told them their check-in time wasn't for two more hours, Nick challenged him by reiterating that they had been traveling for three hours and how he was exhausted after dealing with all the crazy drivers on the road.

Once Nick realized that he couldn't persuade the clerk to let them check into their room early, he yelled, "You need to get your manager right now!"

When the manager appeared a few minutes later, Nick pointed his finger at him and demanded, "You need to be ready to check people into their rooms when they arrive."

Chloe started feeling uneasy. She squeezed Nick's arm. "It isn't worth arguing over. Let's go exploring and get some coffee; it will be fun."

Nick's attention shifted from the manager to Chloe. He quickly took hold of her arm and led her outside, away from any potential eavesdroppers.

"I'm not arguing. I'm discussing this with the manager," he said.

Chloe took on an apologetic tone and said, "It sounded like an argument when you first started raising your voice with the counter clerk."

"You need to grow up and stop worrying about everything," Nick said, his voice cold.

In all their time together, Nick had never spoken to Chloe with such venom. The echo of his whispered promises and countless 'I love yous' mocked her now, a cruel reminder of the tenderness that seemed so distant.

Chloe was dumbfounded. "Why are you saying mean things to me?"

"I wouldn't have to say these things to you if you didn't put me down," Nick answered.

When Chloe covered her mouth to stifle a sob, Nick reacted quickly. Not wanting to risk being viewed as a bad partner if Chloe started crying in public, he decided to distract her from how she was feeling.

"We are both tired from the ride up the mountain," Nick said. "Let's grab something to eat while we wait for our room to be ready."

Once they got into their room, Nick told her, "I always have the best time when I am with you. If the manager hadn't made me so angry, I would have never spoken to you like that. I am so sorry that you got upset."

Nick's apology completely disarmed Chloe. He wanted to make things right, and she didn't want Nick's argument with the hotel staff to ruin their relationship.

Chloe responded, "You are so sweet. I could never be mad at you."

Nick was absolutely determined to secure Chloe's unwavering support, so he didn't waste any time before proposing to her the next day. For their honeymoon, they went back to the resort in the mountains. The honeymoon suite was ready for them, with complimentary champagne on ice this time.

"See?" Nick said to Chloe. "This is how you get good service."

Chloe thought maybe he was right.

Two months into their marriage, Chloe noticed that Nick had a habit of being late whenever they had plans. Initially, she thought he was pre-occupied with work, so she tried different ways to remind him. But when Chloe called him at work, Nick told her it wasn't a good time to talk on the phone. Even when she texted him to confirm the time to meet, Nick would say he didn't have time to check all of her messages. Whenever Chloe asked him if something was going on at work that caused him to be late, Nick would tell her that she got the time wrong.

Chloe sensed a shift in her relationship with Nick right after they returned from their honeymoon. They started spending less time together, and when they were together, something felt off. She tried talking to Nick about her concerns, but he insisted everything was fine.

Chloe decided they needed a date night, and she was determined to make it happen. She made a reservation for dinner at a nice restaurant for Friday night.

Chloe left work early on Friday to take her time getting ready. Once she got home, she took a long bath and did her hair and makeup. She put on a new dress that she had bought, especially for the date. It was a beautiful red dress that hugged her curves perfectly. She added some gold jewelry and her favorite pair of high heels.

Chloe felt a mixture of excitement and nervousness as she tapped the "request ride" button on her phone. She was hopeful that her upcoming date would reignite her connection with Nick and possibly even bring them back to the place they were before they got married.

As Chloe entered the restaurant, the hostess greeted her. "Welcome to Giovanni's Place," she said. "Do you have a reservation?"

"Yes," Chloe said. "The name is Chloe."

The hostess checked her reservation book. "Ah, yes," she said. "Table for two. Right this way."

The hostess led Chloe to a table in the back of the restaurant. The table was secluded and had a view of the city lights.

"Here you are," the hostess said. "Your waiter will be with you shortly."

Chloe took a deep breath and smiled. She was excited to spend a romantic evening with her husband.

A few minutes later, a waiter came to take Chloe's order. "Can I start you off with something to drink?" he asked.

"I'll wait for my husband," Chloe said.

Twenty minutes after Nick was supposed to arrive, Chloe felt herself starting to get nervous. She thought, *What if he doesn't show up?*

Just then, Chloe caught sight of Nick entering the restaurant. He was dressed in a sharp suit and tie, looking quite handsome.

Nick walked over to the table and gave Chloe a kiss. "You look beautiful," he said.

"Thank you," Chloe said. "You don't look so bad yourself."

Once Nick sat down at the table, Chloe said, "I picked this restaurant because I know you like Italian food, and someone at work told me they have the best pasta."

Nick was confused as he listened to Chloe talk. He couldn't understand why she would listen to someone else's opinion without checking with him first to see if the restaurant was a good choice.

Nick gave Chloe a dirty look and then used a lie about having eaten at the restaurant to attack her for not comprehending that his opinion was the most important. "Your friend at work doesn't know what they're talking about. I have eaten here before. The food is terrible. Let's leave."

As they left the restaurant, Nick told Chloe he wanted to pick up some lunch meat from the grocery store for dinner. Chloe agreed and suggested that they could also grab some food for the weekend while they were there.

As they drove to the grocery store, Chloe couldn't stop replaying the restaurant fiasco in her mind. She had been looking forward to a romantic evening with Nick and hoped it would be a chance to reconnect with him, but instead, regret over her restaurant choice had burrowed deep in her gut. Chloe wanted to apologize and try to get their date night back on track, but Nick's silence and tight grip on the steering wheel left her feeling that now was not the right time to discuss things with him.

The automatic doors whooshed open as Chloe and Nick stepped inside the brightly lit grocery store. Nick picked a cart from the row of carts near the entrance and steered it towards the deli, where he joined the line of other customers waiting to be served.

When it was his turn, Nick asked the deli clerk for some ham and roast beef. After he got his order, he began navigating the aisles in the store. Nick bought a Caesar salad kit, canned soup, a pack of marinated wings, and a few bags of chips.

Nick asked Chloe, "Are you going to put anything in the cart?"

Chloe saw the cart was already full of groceries, so she answered, "No, I can't think of anything else that we need."

When they got to the front of the store, Nick noticed that all the checkout lanes had at least three people waiting in line with full carts. But the express checkout only had two customers in line and they were carrying their groceries in small baskets.

Unwilling to wait behind people with large carts full of groceries, Nick pushed his cart toward the express checkout. As Nick approached, one of the customers in line turned around to look at him.

She said, "This is the express checkout for twelve items or less."

In a callous tone, Nick replied, "Why do you think I care what you have to say?"

The lady was shocked by Nick's response. She turned around and finished putting her groceries on the conveyor belt.

Nick stared at the clock on his phone, impatiently watching the seconds tick by while he waited for the lady to put the checkout divider on the conveyor belt. When Nick heard the lady ask for a pack of cigarettes, he expected the cashier would screw up the order and delay his checking out. Feeling annoyed, Nick grabbed a case of water from his shopping cart and slammed it on the conveyor belt.

Hearing the sharp crack of the case of water hitting the conveyor belt, the cashier looked up. After glancing at Nick, she let out a small sigh. Seasoned by years behind the register, the cashier knew she couldn't get him to calm down. So rather than engaging with him, the cashier told Nick this was an express line, but she would take him this time.

The tension from the grocery store continued as Nick stepped inside the apartment, arms overflowing with grocery bags. Nick dumped the bag's contents onto the kitchen counter. Some cans got dented, and a bag of chips crushed, but it didn't seem to matter to Nick. He grabbed the groceries off the counter and shoved them onto the shelves. He crumpled up the empty grocery bags, slammed the cabinet doors shut, and then turned to face Chloe.

"Chloe, you know that I am always here for you. I picked you up from work last week when you had a flat tire. But you are never there for me. It pisses me off that you didn't listen to me. I told you before how much I hated that restaurant. I don't deserve this."

Chloe had hoped that their date night would let her and Nick step away from their routine, allowing them to rediscover the joy of spending time together. Instead, Nick was lashing out at her for not considering him.

A flicker of hurt crossed Chloe's face before being quickly replaced by confusion as she tentatively asked, "What can I do differently to make you happy?"

A sneaky suspicion suddenly popped into Nick's mind that Chloe was trying to control the conversation by questioning him about their relationship. Refusing to let Chloe dominate the conversation, Nick switched gears and pointed out how he was being mistreated.

As Nick spoke, his voice began to rise until he was shouting, and any control he had quickly slipped away. "You're crazy. I don't have the energy to change anybody, and I never said that you needed to be different. You are trying to destroy this family by always trying to start a fight."

Something changed for Chloe at that moment. She knew marriage was work, but she was tired of being blamed for their problems. When she thought about the few times Nick had apologized, it was always for her hurt feelings, not what he had done to cause them.

The following weekend Chloe went to stay with her girlfriend, Jill. She needed to take a break and decide if she was seeing things clearly.

After Chloe got to Jill's house, they ordered a pizza. They sat on the couch and talked while they waited for the pizza to arrive.

Chloe confided in Jill that Nick used to be the perfect partner for her. He would shower her with affection and attention, making her feel like she was the only girl in the world. But now, things had changed. Nick made her feel like a burden and didn't seem to pay attention when she tried to talk to him about how she felt. Instead, he dismissed her concerns by accusing her of being too sensitive or constantly trying to start a fight.

While listening to Chloe, Jill became convinced that Nick was less invested in the marriage than Chloe was. Jill told Chloe that she believed a successful marriage required an unwavering commitment from both partners. But since Jill had never been married, she was hesitant to give any specific advice to Chloe, fearing that it could backfire and make the situation worse.

The texting from Nick started that Friday night after Chloe got to Jill's house. The texts were about how much he missed her and wanted her to come home so they could spend some time together. On Saturday morning, he texted her, telling her he wasn't feeling well. His stomach and head were hurting. When Chloe didn't respond to his texts by lunchtime, Nick told her he loved her.

Chloe had already begun to feel uneasy about being at her friend's house. Even though Jill tried to be supportive, Chloe didn't believe that Jill fully understood what she was going through.

Chloe thought, *Maybe Nick was right. She could be blowing things out of proportion, causing them to fight.* Even so, she didn't understand why Nick got so angry.

Nick continued to text: "I need you to come home and take care of me."

Chloe told Jill that Nick wasn't feeling well, so she had to cut her visit short. Trying to be a supportive friend, Jill said that she understood, but at the same time, she couldn't help but wonder if Nick was manipulating Chloe.

As soon as Chloe returned home, Nick began accusing her, "I know that you told your friend bad things about me."

Chloe had expected her weekend with Jill to be a great way to relax and recharge, but now Nick was demanding an apology from her for seeking out support from her friend.

Chloe responded to Nick's accusations: "I just wanted to have a girls' weekend."

Nick lashed out at Chloe. "It's not fair that you put your friend ahead of me. But that's okay because you will never find anybody who loves you like me. I am the best friend that you will ever have."

Chloe felt like her life was quickly spinning out of control. "You make it sound like I am the devil incarnate. I don't know what to believe anymore."

Nick stepped up his accusations. "You are a drama queen. I don't have time for your games. I love you, but I don't understand why you are so set on destroying our family."

Nick made Chloe feel foolish. Foolish for doubting herself and foolish for thinking her thoughts mattered to him. Chloe realized that she would never see some things in the same way as Nick.

Feeling overwhelmed by the toxic environment at home, Chloe began spending more time at work. When her boss chose her to lead a project, Chloe quickly identified all the steps needed to complete the project on time. Her problem-solving skills impressed her team, and they praised her for her exceptional work. This recognition was particularly meaningful to Chloe, as it made her see herself differently than the way Nick made her feel. Nick had tried to make her believe she needed to question her judgment because, according to him, she was always missing something.

Nick noticed that Chloe was changing. Not only was she spending less time at home, but she also didn't seem as interested in what was going on in his life.

When Chloe didn't ask enough questions about a story Nick was telling, he pointed out, "You don't care about this family. I need you, but you aren't there for me."

Chloe decided that something had to change. She was tired of being accused of not doing enough and feeling like she was walking on eggshells around Nick.

Chloe looked at Nick, her eyes filling with tears. "I always loved you even when you gave me so many reasons not to. Two of the saddest words are, 'If only.' If only you had taken the blame just once for the problems in our relationship, we might have had a chance at being happy."

Nick refused to continue the conversation with Chloe and didn't speak to her again for over a week. Chloe tried to get Nick to talk to her, but he wouldn't until one day when he drove to Chloe's job and called her on his cell phone from the parking lot. He had something that he wanted to give her.

When Nick saw Chloe approaching his car, he rolled down the window. He handed Chloe some papers without saying anything to her.

Chloe stood alone in the parking lot, watching Nick drive away. As Nick merged onto the street, he cut off a driver, causing the car to swerve into another lane.

When the driver blew his horn at Nick, Nick yelled out the window, "Learn to drive, moron."

The weight of the papers Nick had given Chloe felt heavy in her hands. Their crisp edges dug into her skin like accusations. Even before she unfolded them, she knew what they were—divorce papers.

The reality of the situation hit hard and sent a tremor through Chloe's body, but it was accompanied by the relief of never having to question her sanity again. Nick had almost convinced her that the problems in their marriage were all her fault and that she was "crazy."

With a determined glint in her eyes, Chloe slipped her wedding ring into her pocket. She squared her shoulders, took a deep breath, and turned towards her office building. Chloe realized that this wasn't the end. It was a new beginning, one where she would write her own story.

THE MAN IS THE REASON

Crowning the bike's sturdy frame was a set of high-rise ape hanger handlebars stretching out like an eagle's wings, poised for flight. Beneath this commanding perch, a long and low banana seat promised a ride of effortless comfort and unadulterated pleasure. This eye-catching combination was guaranteed to turn heads and set hearts racing.

The bike wasn't exactly fresh from the factory, but Frank's uncle had breathed new life into it with a coat of metallic blue paint on the frame and a set of new tires. Frank was grateful to his uncle because he knew his parents couldn't afford to buy him a bike, even a secondhand one.

Today, Frank had his final initiation into the Hill Side Players. The rules of the initiation were simple but challenging. He had to reach the bottom of the quarry in less than two minutes and then climb back up the same treacherous path in less than four minutes. The distance itself was not the problem; it was the sheer verticality of the quarry face that made it a daunting test of skill and courage.

Frank was ready for his chance. He was eagerly waiting with the bike between his legs. Frank heard someone yell, "Ready!" He lifted his right foot off the ground and put it on the pedal. He heard, "Set." He leaned into the handlebars, pushing the bike forward.

On "Go," the flag dropped. Frank pushed off with his left foot and pressed down on the pedal with his right foot as hard as he could.

Becoming a Player was something that Frank had dreamed of for as long as he could remember. Even before he owned a bike, he would spend countless hours at the quarry, watching the Players practice their stunts.

One of his favorite stunts was when the bikes would jump over a rock wall the miners had built when the quarry first opened. It was impossible to know for sure how the bikes would hit the ground. Some bikes would hit with both wheels, but the best landings were when the back tire hit the ground first, sending a small cloud of dust into the air.

Frank rolled across the finish line. He had made it to the bottom of the quarry in less than two minutes and back to the top in less than three minutes. Frank wished that his uncle could see him now. Frank was eleven years old and a Player.

Frank's childhood unfolded in a working-class neighborhood, where towering smokestacks cast long shadows over the horizon, and the rhythmic clang of machinery provided a constant backdrop to life. His family rented a small, three-bedroom house on the outskirts of town. The house was modest, with peeling paint and creaky floorboards.

Despite Frank's father working at the tool factory and his mother working as a waitress at the local diner, money was always tight. The major cause of their financial problems was Frank's father's inability to get along with people. He frequently got into arguments with his neighbors, friends, and even his own family.

Frank's father was known for his favorite phrase: "well, actually." He liked to use it when telling people how to live their lives. A person could be talking about something as mundane as having picked out which television show to watch that night, and Frank's father would inject his wisdom beginning with, *well, actually. Well, actually,* you should watch the other show. It's better.

Frank's father's know-it-all attitude and condescending demeanor made it difficult for him to build strong relationships with his boss or coworkers. It was never a surprise to any of the workers at the tool factory that Frank's father was frequently the first one to be laid off when things were slow at the factory.

Arguments about money often became violent between Frank's parents when his father's unemployment would run out. By the time he was eleven, Frank had seen his mother with a busted lip at least half a dozen times.

The Hill Side Players were Frank's only saving grace from his problem at home. For them, the quarry was not just a place to test their limits and defy gravity; it let them escape the grief of their home lives—violence and neglect.

While the Hill Side Players were bound by an unbreakable bond of brotherhood, they were also fiercely competitive with each other. They would race their bikes, challenge each other in video games, and compete for the highest score in bowling. But their favorite competition was pinball.

Each time it was Frank's turn to play, he would insert his hard-earned quarters in the pinball machine, representing the countless hours he had spent mowing lawns, shoveling snow, and running errands for his neighbors. Frank would try to extend his playtime each time he pressed a flipper and every pinball bounce because he knew asking his parents for money was out of the question, and there were only so many opportunities for an eleven-year-old to get some cash. Frank didn't win the title for the highest score in pinball, but the Players did give him a title for keeping the ball in play for the longest time.

One day, when Frank was in the fourth grade, he was walking down the school hallway holding his bathroom pass. In passing, he overheard a conversation between a teacher and an office staff member about his family's financial struggles. The teacher noticed Frank listening and asked why he wasn't in class. Frank showed his pass to the teacher and headed toward the restroom.

After hearing the teacher and staff member gossip about his family and witnessing the teacher's dismissive attitude toward him when he got caught eavesdropping, Frank began to assume that when an adult at school looked at him like he was dirty or had a negative attitude towards him, it was because he was different; he was poor.

Despite being judged by some of his teachers as the boy from the wrong side of town, with tattered clothes and haunted eyes, Frank refused to let their preconceived notions define him. At school, he found solace in the rustle of turning pages, the secrets of history, and the intricate dance of equations.

However, Frank would let his mind wander if the material was boring or the teacher's monotone voice wasn't engaging. Bored by a history lesson, Frank's mind became a time machine. His father walks in the back door of their house, wearing a suit and tie. He gives Frank a high five and tells him the whole family is going out for pizza to celebrate his promotion at work.

Frank liked escaping in his mind to a place where his father was a better man and he was living in a happy family, but Frank knew that daydreaming would not solve any of his problems. The only other way Frank knew how to deal with his problems was to ignore them, just like his parents did.

Frank was able to ignore the possibility that his family might run out of food or be forced to move in with his grandmother until he was in the 8th grade, and his father asked him if he could spare five dollars for lunch at work. On that day, Frank lost a lot of respect for his father. After his father asked for money for the second time, Frank knew he did not want to be anything like his father, someone you could not depend on.

The sting of poverty left a deep emotional scar on Frank's young mind. However, he didn't let it defeat him. Instead, he used it as a driving force to achieve financial success. For Frank, being wealthy simply meant not constantly struggling, fearing unexpected bills, or feeling vulnerable and unseen. Financial success was not only a practical necessity but also a personal validation. It was a way for Frank to prove his worth and rewrite the narrative of his past.

After graduating from college, Frank received three job offers, and he chose the one that paid the most. He believed that the more money he had, the fewer people would have control over his life.

Three years later, Frank was promoted to department manager, a position he hoped would protect him from the emotional turmoil he had witnessed in his parents' relationship. He believed that having enough money would prevent arguments, anxieties, and the erosion of love in his romantic relationships.

Feeling confident, Frank proposed to Abigail, the woman who had captured his heart since college. He was sure that his family would never have to face the hardships he did as a child.

Frank's salary provided a comfortable life for his family, but his new management position came with a lot of responsibility. To keep track of everything and ensure smooth functioning, the department managers had to attend a mandatory meeting with Jeff, the managing director, every Monday.

Shortly after Frank moved into his new management position, he requested additional personnel to assist with an upcoming project. However, Jeff responded by accusing Frank of not knowing how to manage his team. He demanded that Frank complete a review of every job description and salary in his department, starting with an outline of Frank's responsibilities. Jeff wanted to ensure the company wasn't paying people more than they were worth.

The extra work, added to Frank's already busy schedule, caused him to miss one of the Monday management meetings. Frank heard through the grapevine that Jeff had gotten belligerent in the meeting after one of the department managers brought up his concerns about a selected vendor on an upcoming project. Jeff told the manager he was about as much use as an old dog sitting under a porch licking his balls.

After hearing how Jeff had acted in the meeting, Frank considered resigning. The fact that Jeff had already shown that he always had to be right and was never satisfied with anyone else's ideas made Frank wonder just how far Jeff's disrespect might go with him. Frank knew Jeff might not give him a good reference, but his heart told him to start looking for a new job.

Frank was torn about quitting his job with his family depending on him financially. Long ago, Frank promised himself that his children would never have to experience getting secondhand presents, like the second-hand bike his uncle got him when he was eleven years old. Still, he found it tough to deal with Jeff being disrespectful.

Frank considered talking to Abigail about his work concerns, but he couldn't figure out where to begin—the last time he could remember being open about his feelings had been when he was a kid in the Hill Side Players. He told one of the other Players how much he hated it when he had to listen to his parents fighting. That had been so long ago.

Frank reverted to his "real man" mentality. He buried his emotions inside so he wouldn't come off as weak. When Abigail asked about work, Frank played down how he felt by saying everything was fine.

Try as he might, Frank couldn't decide if Jeff's blatant disrespect was because he was seeking attention or didn't know himself. Either way, Frank never had the unrealistic expectation that his boss would like him or that a person has to necessarily like their job. But still, having to keep his guard up against his boss because he was quick to turn on people wasn't okay.

The turmoil at work left Frank feeling raw and on edge. The only way that Frank knew how to communicate his emotions was through actions. These actions showed up as angry outbursts grossly disproportionate to the situation.

Frank threw a magazine across the room when his wife told him he needed to meet her at the garage and give her a ride to work. The brake pads on the car had to be replaced.

One of the guys at work changed a password on one of the computers. Frank lashed out at him and called him an idiot.

Frank's reactions made him doubt his ability to be the support Abigail deserved or someone his colleagues could respect. He had never wanted to be like his father, someone who would lash out with fists or a demeaning attitude, so he began looking for an outlet for his pent-up emotions.

Spending more time at the gym became Frank's refuge. The gym helped to chip away at his anxiety, but he still needed to figure out how to keep from coming up short.

An old childhood memory kept playing in Frank's mind. He and another boy sat on their bikes at the starting line, ready to race down the quarry.

The other boy looked at Frank with a cocky smile and said, "You're going to lose this race."

The other kid's bike was newer and the most likely winner from the start, but Frank's friend, Marty, had kept him from feeling too bad by snarkily blaming the other kid's winning on his good luck. Thinking about Marty made Frank believe that somebody else might be able to give him some pointers on how to negotiate his feelings of self-respect at work.

Frank decided to take a chance and talk to his friend Dale. Dale had been his spotting partner at the gym now for over six years.

Frank finished spotting Dale with his third set of bench presses. He took a deep breath and said, "I'm not really sure what I'm supposed to be doing at this point in my life."

Dale paused. He had seen his brother express this degree of heartfelt emotion when his wife asked him for a divorce. Even then, he didn't want to respond in way that would be seen as too caring. He didn't want to be judged as weak. On the other hand, if he acted like he didn't care at all, then he would be seen as a dick.

Dale opted for: "Just try harder. Whatever's going on is a phase. It will pass."

Frank understood that Dale was focused on fixing the problem. Frank would have done the same thing. Frank never wanted or needed anyone to fix any of his problems. This time, he just wanted someone to listen and take his side.

The conversation ended with Dale saying, "What happened to you? You were always a fighter. So go ahead and man up."

The armor came up for Frank. He buried his feelings and doubled down at work. He took all emotion out of the equation and relied on logic in all his decision-making.

Frank's commitment to keeping his emotional armor on at work unintentionally impacted his ability to connect with his family. His constant effort to protect himself during work hours drained his energy, leaving him barely enough stamina to engage with his family when he was home.

Abigail responded to the growing distance between her and her husband by asking Frank why he was shutting her out. She accused him of being emotionally unavailable.

The words "emotionally unavailable" made Frank cringe. His wife was pointing out the obvious—his inability to express his emotions was affecting their relationship. Yet, Frank was doing his best.

Frank wasn't sure what to do. He had started with a plan to get where he needed to be, but now everything seemed uncertain. He was making money and had a wife whom he loved, but he was still falling short.

Frank decided to try talking to someone about how he was feeling just one more time. He approached his friend Logan as they left the gym.

"My wife is becoming resentful about all the time I spend in my man cave," Frank said.

"I spend a lot of time in my man cave," Logan said. "Especially when my wife wants to know what I'm thinking about."

"I get what you're saying," Frank said. "Sometimes, I don't know what I should say."

"We aren't machines," Logan said. "It's a big shift from being ruthless at work to being all touchy-feely at home. It's like we are expected to fix everything at work and home."

"I've always pushed this down because I thought I was the only one who felt like that," Frank said.

"Trust me, Frank," Logan said. "You are not the only one wondering if he will ever be good enough."

After listening to Logan, Frank realized that he had always been afraid that he would come up short, even if he did everything perfectly. His demons were very persuasive when they whispered his greatest fear in his ear, "You'll never have what it takes. Just look at your father, arrogant and abusive."

For years, Frank had tried to bury his demons deep down inside, but they were always there, lurking just beneath the surface, waiting for the moment when they could break free. He couldn't outrun them; they were a part of him. He had to face them, to confront them head-on.

Looking into his demon's cold, dead eyes, Frank saw a six-year-old version of himself who was so insecure. In the reflection, he saw himself hiding in his bedroom while his father yelled at his mother. Frank listened to his father getting angrier and angrier and wondered if he had to be angry when he was a man.

Frank would ask himself: What if I don't want to be angry all the time? What if I don't want to have problems getting along with people?

Frank wondered if his father had been more positive and less negative, then maybe he wouldn't have been the first to get laid off at his job, and then maybe he wouldn't have hit his mother.

But the biggest question Frank had was: If I don't want to be like my father, am I good enough to be any different?

Frank was thinking about his father, but his thoughts soon shifted to his work. He couldn't help but notice the similarities between his father and Jeff. His father would push his mother around whenever he was confronted with the fact that he was an unreliable man, and Jeff was quick to belittle others whenever he felt threatened by them. Frank now saw them both for who they truly were: cowardly individuals who sought control over other people as a substitute for true courage.

Frank finally knew that he wasn't anything like his father. He wasn't anything like his boss. He had never been stoked about controlling other people's lives. He was only concerned about fewer people having control over his life.

Frank realized that moving forward had to be about more than putting his demons to rest. He wanted to try to explain himself to his wife, but he was uncertain about how much he should share. He didn't want to give his wife a reason to judge him as less of a man.

Frank searched his heart for the right words to express his feelings before finally saying, "I would never want you to be disappointed in me or feel like I let you down."

Abigail reassured him: "If something is bothering you, you can talk to me about it."

Frank continued, "I want you to know that you have been a part of everything good in my life."

Abigail looked into Frank's eyes and confessed, "I have loved you since the moment we shared our first kiss."

All of Frank's armor melted away.

"What would be the one thing that I could do to destroy our marriage?"

Abigail wasn't sure where the conversation was going, but she knew the answer instinctively.

"That's an easy one. It would be infidelity."

Frank was starting to feel uncomfortable sharing his thoughts, but he knew he was too far in to back out now.

"Do you want to know the one thing you could do to destroy our marriage?"

"Of course I do," Abigail answered.

Frank took a deep breath to help him summon his courage.

"I may not want to discuss my feelings in depth for hours at a time, but there may be a time when I need a sounding board. If I ever confess that I feel like I came up short, and you use my confession of coming up short to attack my masculinity, then that would be an unforgivable thing for me. That would mean that I couldn't trust you. Like fidelity is a trust issue with you."

Abigail recognized that trust can be interpreted differently by men and women. Infidelity, for her, would be more emotionally damaging, as it would imply sharing intimate moments with someone else that should have been exclusively shared with her. Abigail also understood that using her husband's vulnerability against him could be catastrophic. It could cause him to feel attacked and lead to him shutting down or avoiding conversations altogether.

Abigail's assurance was genuine as she said, "I understand what you're saying. You can trust me. I have believed in you since the first time we kissed."

Sharing some of his burdens with his wife helped Frank understand himself better. He knew things might still go wrong, but that didn't make him a failure. The reality is that one person can't fix everything.

Besides, even if his demons tried to convince him that he had come up short, Frank knew he could shrug it off because he had found a sanctuary where he could be vulnerable without fear of judgment. Abigail's reassuring words were a beacon of light that would always be there whenever the demons tried to pull him back into the abyss.

THE AMBIANCE

As you step through the arched doorway, your senses are immediately engulfed by the mouthwatering aroma of freshly baked bread and cured meats. The warm and inviting air embraces you, and your eyes are treated to a colorful sight of shelves lined with jars filled with olives, pickled vegetables, and pasta sauces. The sweet scent of freshly baked pastries tickles your nose, and you can't resist taking a peek at the counter. Behind it, the meat slicers tirelessly hum, expertly slicing through succulent meats and cheeses with perfect precision. Etched on the front of the counter in bold red, white, and green letters is "Nikko's Deli."

When Victor and Joe were young, their parents used to take them to Nikko's. And now, even after retiring a year ago, their wives still sent them there every Friday.

Today, Victor and Joe were headed to Nikko's to buy all the special treats their families wanted for the weekend. Victor was shopping for some biscotti for dipping in coffee and fresh mozzarella for the Caprese salad for Sunday dinner. Joe wanted to buy some fresh bread and ham. Some of his kids were coming over to the house on Saturday, and it was a tradition to eat sandwiches while they watched the ballgames on television.

When Victor and Joe arrived, they were surprised that the parking lot was already packed. Victor found a spot after circling the parking lot a few times. Joe was not so fortunate; he had to park on the street.

After spending over fifteen minutes looking for a parking spot, Victor and Joe knew the sheer volume of people would make navigating the store challenging. They opted for the convenience of the motorized shopping carts to make maneuvering through the aisles easier.

As the men entered the store, Joe grabbed a motorized cart and went to the left. Victor drove his cart to the right.

Victor and Joe arrived at the deli counter at the same time. When they saw each other, Joe clenched his jaw, and Victor shook his head.

The deli clerk asked, "Who's next?"

Victor and Joe both answered simultaneously, "I am."

The deli clerk attempted to settle the matter. "Who was here first?"

Both men answered, "Me."

Victor glared at Joe. His face was turning red.

Joe raised his eyebrows and pointed his finger at Victor. "You got this wrong."

The next thing everyone knew, the men drove their shopping carts at each other. The carts hit, the carts backed up, and the carts hit again. Each time the carts hit, the men would threaten each other.

Joe pounded his fists on his chest, his knuckles turning white, as he said, "You want a piece of me. Come on, try it."

Victor stuck his hand out, his index finger crooked into a beckoning gesture, and said, "Hit my cart one more time. I'll teach you some respect."

Nikko was sitting in his office, reviewing the day's sales figures, when suddenly, the usual hum of the store was replaced with a mix of shouts and a loud bang. As Nikko came out to see what all the commotion was about, he saw two old guys getting ready to get off their motorized carts and fight each other.

When Nikko realized neither of the men would back down, he got two deli clerks to come out to where the men sat in their motorized carts to take their orders. Nikko told them their orders were on the house, but they would both need to leave the store. Nikko offered to walk them out to their cars so he would know where they were parked and could personally bring their orders to their vehicles once they were ready.

The banging of the carts wasn't only about who got to the deli counter first. There was some history between Victor and Joe. They had grown up on the same street. Their wives were good friends, and their children were close in age.

When Victor's daughter, Maria, was in the third grade, she was on the gymnastics team and qualified for the semifinals with her balance bar routine. The regional championship was in a different state, so the coach had everyone on the team sell cookies to raise money for the trip.

One Friday night, when Maria found out that Joe and his family were coming to dinner, she asked her father, "Dad, can I ask Joe to buy a box of my cookies?"

Victor replied, "Sure, sweetie. Everyone likes cookies."

After dinner, Maria asked Joe to buy a box of her cookies, and he answered, "Why would I pay three dollars for a box of your cookies when I can go to the store and get a bigger bag for a buck-fifty?"

Joe's response made Maria tear up. She had known Joe all her life and was confused about why he had responded so abruptly.

Victor was furious at Joe for upsetting Maria. Joe had the money but had to drill it down for the little girl. So, at that moment, Victor decided the days of doing anything else with Joe were over.

After the cookie incident, Victor and Joe didn't speak to each other again for over twenty years. But, recently, they had joined the same retirement group in their neighborhood. The group met every weekday morning at a local coffee shop.

Each morning, Victor and Joe would order and pay for their coffee and pastries at the cash register. After receiving their receipt, they would take it to the counter and wait for their order to be made.

Victor and Joe used their time wisely while waiting for their espresso or cappuccino. They would scan the restaurant to see where the other one was sitting so they could avoid sitting next to each other if possible. If not, the conversations generally started civilly but often ended with one of them leaving.

One week after the fight with the motorized shopping carts, fate would have it that the only empty seat available was the one next to Joe. As Victor sat down, he heard Joe ranting about how a homeless man outside the coffee shop had approached him and asked if he could spare a few dollars.

Joe had proven himself to be such a tightwad with Maria over a box of cookies that Victor couldn't resist taking a jab at him.

"Did you at least give him some change?"

Ignoring the question, Joe scooted his chair away from Victor's seat and continued with his tirade. "All these homeless people seem to have dogs. I couldn't believe how big that guy's dog was. Just imagine how much food that dog would eat and how expensive it would be. The man would be better off if he got rid of the dog. Then, he could get a job and stop begging for money on the street."

As Joe talked about how a dog could lead a person to become homeless, Victor watched through the restaurant window as the homeless man scratched his dog's head.

"He seems to genuinely care about his dog," Victor said. "The guy is probably just down on his luck."

Listening to Victor talk only agitated Joe. "These homeless guys aren't down on their luck. I have seen them pull up in their cars and go into the church for a free meal."

Joe seemed more interested in imposing his point of view than engaging in a genuine dialogue, so Victor asked, "Should a homeless guy be forced to sell his car before he can get something to eat? You know a car can be a lifeline for a homeless person. It can provide them with a place to sleep and a way to get to work, which can help them get back on their feet."

Joe thought Victor was trying to be slick, disguising his attack on him by asking ridiculous questions. Joe pushed to his feet and slammed his chair under the table. He gave Victor a threatening look and stormed out of the restaurant.

After Joe left, all the other guys sitting at the table turned their heads toward Victor. No words were spoken, but they all understood that Joe had a narrow-minded attitude. He was adamant about his own beliefs and never considered any alternate point of view.

The following Monday at the coffee shop, Joe was sullen. His sister had called him over the weekend to tell him that his nephew had announced at dinner on Friday night that he was gay.

The unexpected news hit Joe like a punch to the gut. He had always envisioned his nephew marrying a woman, having children, and building a traditional family life. Now, that image was shattered, replaced with an unfamiliar reality.

Angry at his nephew for not being the person he had always thought he was, Joe said, "My nephew thinks he's gay. I want to find him and beat some sense into him. Getting hit in the head a few times should tighten up all those loose screws."

Everyone at the table looked at Joe, then back and forth between each other as they exchanged surprised glances. They couldn't reconcile Joe's violent attitude toward gay people with how much he enjoyed bragging to everyone that his nephew already had a job lined up while he was still in his last semester in college.

After realizing some people were staring at him, Joe defensively said, "I just want him to tell me why he's gay."

Victor knew that sexual orientation is not something that can be explained or chosen. It was simply an integral part of who someone is.

Trying to help Joe understand that being gay is simply one way to be human, Victor asked, "What if your nephew wanted you to explain to him why you dreamed what you dreamed last night?"

Joe rubbed the back of his neck, trying to release some of the tension he felt from being questioned about his relationship with his nephew.

"What are you talking about? Look, you don't have to be disrespectful."

Victor replied: "I'm not disrespecting you; it's just how you let your beliefs cloud your thoughts about your nephew."

Everyone quickly finished their coffee, made excuses, and left.

Since Joe was a child, he tended to paint people different from him with a broad brush. It was an attitude of us versus them for Joe.

Joe's retired coffee-drinking buddies were the single exception to his rules. Joe tolerated some of their differences because many of the guys in the group liked the same sports teams as he did, and he enjoyed playing Monday morning quarterback with them after a game.

All of Joe's other friends were just like him. They believed they were the only ones who knew the truth and that their ideology would solve the world's problems. As a result, Joe and his other like-minded friends quickly confirmed each other's beliefs that everyone else was wrong.

The next day, Joe's visit to the coffee shop was like every other day. He found a way to look down on someone who didn't fit into his narrow mold.

He began his tirade, "I was accosted by some Black college kid on the street."

Victor was in no mood to listen to exaggerations. "What are you talking about anyway?"

Joe turned away from Victor and crossed his arms before saying, "This kid walks up to me on the street and asks me to participate in his survey. I said sure, as long as it wouldn't take too long. He asked me if I knew what equality or discrimination meant. I told him that, of course, I knew what words in the dictionary meant. I asked him if he knew what 'swimming with the fishes' meant."

"He's a kid to all of us old guys," Victor exclaimed. "It would help if you gave him a break."

Constantly feeling as if he had to defend himself, Joe became angry. "This kid didn't deserve a break! He accused me of exerting my white privilege while I talked to him."

Victor asked, "Do you even know what white privilege is?"

Joe snapped back, "It's the idea that white people had everything handed to them!"

Victor asked, "Are you sure?"

Joe answered, "Yeah, I'm sure!"

Victor paused for a moment, taking a deep breath to calm the frustration building up inside him. He realized that arguing with Joe would only aggravate the situation, so he decided to take a different approach.

"Remember when we were kids?" Victor reminisced, a smile on his face. "We used to make our way uptown to that two-story candy store. We only had thirty-five cents in our pocket back then, so we had to be very picky about what we bought. We would spend an hour in the store and only walk out with two pieces of candy.

"What about when the two Black kids walked out of the store behind us? We thought we were about to get mugged because we remembered everything our parents told us about Black people being criminals. But, lucky for us, those two kids went a different direction than us; they weren't following us after all.

"Or do you remember when we had our fake IDs that summer after high school? We went to the club up on 10th Avenue. That was another time we thought we would get jumped by some Black guys. Come to find out, those guys just wanted to know the bartender's name.

"White privilege is being able to go into a store without being followed around like you are going to steal something or not having someone say I'll wait on the next elevator because they are afraid to get in a small space with you. Can you imagine someone looking at you like you were a pariah or not wanting to sit close to you just because of your skin color?"

Joe stared at Nick, his anger boiling inside him. "Let me get this straight. Are you telling me that I'm supposed to have a debate about what is or isn't racist with every person of color that I meet? Just to prove that I understand the issue?"

Victor explained, "I'm suggesting being more mindful of your actions and questioning if your beliefs align with reality."

Joe gave Victor a dirty look for assuming he wanted his unsolicited advice. "I'm aware of everything that I do. The good news is I don't have to sit here and let you disrespect me."

Victor replied, "I'm not disrespecting you, just some of your ideas."

Joe pushed his chair back and stood up. He left the restaurant, leaving a full cup of coffee and an uneaten pastry on the table.

The conversation about the value of life proved to be the most consequential. Victor's older brother had been out of work for two years while battling cancer. His family was helping him pay his mortgage and health insurance, so when their doctor recommended an experimental cancer treatment, there wasn't enough money to cover the cost.

Staring down at his cup of coffee, Victor said, "My brother shouldn't have to choose between selling his house and saving his life."

Joe couldn't resist offering some advice. He piped up, "I think the trick is to choose the right insurance plan."

As the words "cold-hearted bastard" hovered on the tip of Victor's tongue, he paused, his eyes narrowing into slits. He knew that calling Joe a cold-hearted bastard would not be enough. He had to do something more, something that would leave a lasting mark on his soul. He decided to make sure Joe understood that he was not immune to the hardships of life.

"Someone in your family could end up in the same spot as my brother. They could work their whole life and still not be able to afford the medical care they need to fight for their life."

Remembering the permanence and irreversibility of death made Joe pause. He had always wished he could talk to his brother again after losing him in a car crash. He realized he was a little resentful that Victor still had a brother, and this made him feel small.

Joe looked down at his cup of coffee on the table and said, "I'm sorry about your brother."

The shock of hearing what Joe said made Victor pause. He was furious with Joe, but after reflecting on the situation, he realized his true anger stemmed from his helplessness in his brother's situation.

"Even if we don't see eye to eye about everything, I still appreciate what you said about my brother," Victor admitted.

For a fleeting moment, Joe's expression clouded with uncertainty, his mind grappling with the unanticipated twist in the narrative. Then, a wave of realization washed over him, settling into a quiet acknowledgment, "Perhaps I don't know as much as I thought I did."

After Joe admitted that he didn't have all the answers, Victor felt hopeful that Joe finally recognized the impact his behavior had on the people around him. But still, Victor took a deep breath and examined Joe's facial expressions, searching for any sign that he might be hiding something.

After Victor didn't pick up any cues that he couldn't trust Joe, he said, "I often think about how humans instinctively put things into categories. For example, we put cats and dogs in the animal category. That's because they have four legs and a tail and are covered in fur.

"We also put people into categories. Remember the homeless man that you were so furious at the other day? You didn't see him as an individual who might be down on his luck. Instead, you categorized him with all homeless people: lazy about work and trying to cheat the system for a handout.

"Remember how you thought you could beat the gayness out of your nephew? Or the Black kids we thought were criminals who wanted to harm us.

"It's important to stop and realize that there are good and bad Black guys and gay guys. It isn't the fact that they are gay or Black that makes them good or bad. It's about how they treat other people that makes them good or bad."

Joe said, "You seem to have given this a lot of thought."

Victor knew it was important to acknowledge that he didn't know everything and to show that vulnerability was okay, so he said, "I'm human and make mistakes every day. Even when I try to put myself in someone else's shoes, I don't always get it right."

Joe realized how unreasonable his attitudes towards certain people had been. Nevertheless, he was grateful that Victor hadn't given up on him. What had it been—twenty years?

"You're right about what you're saying," Joe said. "Who am I to tell people how to live? It's not like I will step into their lives and accept the consequences of my advice."

Victor appreciated Joe's honest appraisal of himself. He knew there had been times in his own life when it had been hard to admit that he was wrong.

"All I ever wanted was for you to consider how you treat people who are different than you. You always had a good heart; you just had to find it inside yourself."

Joe said, "Let's hope time proves you right."

"Let's sit together tomorrow morning while we drink our coffee," Victor said. "We have a lot to catch up on."

Joe replied, "For sure, I look forward to it."

AFTER THE EVENT

The party at the lake was in full swing. Music was blasting from the speakers, drinks were flowing, and the laughter was contagious. Cars were parked on both sides of the road, and people were spilling out of them, eager to join the festivities.

The party had started as an invite-only event for the graduating seniors, but after word of mouth kicked in, it quickly became a massive group of people coming together for an all-out bash. Jocks, nerds, preps, and goths were all rubbing shoulders, having a good time.

As Teresa and Joey stepped out of their car, they were immediately greeted by the sound of music and laughter. Teresa walked over to the bonfire and joined some girls dancing. She laughed and sang along to the music and even made a few new friends. Meanwhile, Joey and his friends stood by the beer keg and talked about baseball games, both the good and the bad. They laughed about the time their team lost to the worst team in the league and reminisced about the time they won the state championship.

As Teresa was standing by the bonfire, a familiar song started playing. It was a secret soundtrack that she and Joey shared, which reminded her of their long-lasting friendship. Teresa and Joey had been best friends since childhood. They grew up together, attended the same schools, and even lived on the same street. Throughout the years, they shared everything, from their deepest secrets to their most embarrassing moments. Each verse of the song brought back memories of their adventures, secrets, and laughter.

After the song finished, Teresa was eager to find Joey. She maneuvered through the party until she finally spotted him sitting on top of a picnic table by the lake.

Teresa walked over to where Joey was seated and sat down beside him. She rested her feet on the bench and looked around. Teresa and Joey had spent a lot of time at the lake when they were children and had sat in this spot many times before.

As the friends sat side by side, their gazes were fixed on the tiny ripples in the water as they chased each other toward the shore. The ripples brought back different memories, from skipping stones across the lake to the nights spent trying to understand the news that one of them had broken up with the person they were dating. As they were reminiscing about the days spent growing up together, Teresa remembered one time that had been especially funny.

"Remember when we mixed up everything we could find in the refrigerator door? It was mustard, buttermilk, ketchup, and hot sauce."

Joey remembered. It smelled like spoiled milk and looked like it had balls of brown snot floating around in a greenish-brown liquid.

"Yeah, Ernie believed us when we told him that we had invented a new dipping sauce for pickles," Joey said. "I remember you putting three dill pickles on a plate for him. He dipped the first one in the sauce and said it tasted good. He ate all three pickles and was out of school with a stomachache for the next two days."

Teresa was laughing but serious when she said, "We did a lot of crazy shit as kids, but I always knew that you had my back."

"I wouldn't have it any other way," Joey replied. "You can always count on me, just like I know I can count on you."

After one of their friends yelled for them to come back and join the party, Teresa and Joey walked back to the bonfire. As everyone gathered around the fire, they discussed their post-high school plans. Most seniors were leaving home to attend college, while others chose to stay in their parents' basements and work at local stores. Joey and Teresa, however, had decided to join the military to serve their country and see the world.

Just before sunrise, Teresa and Joey returned to the same picnic table they had been sitting on earlier. As they sat there, time seemed to lose its meaning. They were lost in a world of their own, a world where happiness and innocence reigned supreme.

Teresa turned to Joey and said, "It's so magical here."

Joey smiled and said, "It's one of my favorite places."

Teresa and Joey sat huddled together, their eyes fixed on the horizon, waiting for the sun to rise. As the first rays of dawn appeared, the sky transformed into a canvas of vibrant hues. Below, the lake became a mirror to the sky, its surface ablaze with pinks and oranges. When the reflections of the surrounding trees started to shimmer and sway in the water, Teresa and Joey suddenly remembered that they had to finish getting their backpacks ready so their parents could drop them off at the bus station.

Joey sat in the window seat as the bus pulled out of the station, listening to Teresa snoring. Although tired from last night's party, Joey couldn't relax. He stared out the window, worrying how his small-town life would compare to the big world. Mostly, he didn't want anything to change between Teresa and himself.

The bus rumbled to a halt next to an immense flag snapping in the wind, its stars a stark contrast to the endless blue sky. Teresa and Joey swallowed, a knot of nervous anticipation tightening in their stomach as they stepped off the bus and into the whirlwind of activity.

As they walked towards the processing center, a lone figure emerged from the shadows of a hangar. A sergeant, his face etched with desert lines and his eyes hard as flint, stood before them. He looked Teresa and Joey up and down, his gaze stripping them bare.

"Welcome to the base, recruits," he said, his voice a gravel rasp. "This is where you'll learn to fight, to bleed, and to die. You'll learn to be a soldier, or you'll wash out. Are you ready?"

With a final nod of encouragement, Teresa and Joey parted ways. Teresa joined her fellow female recruits as they were ushered toward a designated area. Joey found himself amidst a sea of testosterone-fueled camaraderie as he joined his all-male platoon.

After months of rigorous physical and mental training, Teresa and Joey stood tall and proud, having completed basic training. They were at the top of their game in situational awareness and had proven they could perform under extreme stress through combat arms training and field exercises.

Excited to be reunited with Teresa, Joey couldn't wait to catch up with her and tell her everything that happened in the last few months. He had an exciting story to share with her about his time on guard duty in the annex.

"One night, a sergeant started pounding on the door, demanding I let him into the building. When I asked to see his ID card, he flashed it too quickly to see. When I asked to see his ID card again, the sergeant started pushing me to let him in. After a few minutes of going back and forth, he showed his ID card again, but the picture showed a different man with a cigarette hanging out of his mouth. I could have gotten into a lot of trouble if I had opened the door."

Teresa couldn't stop laughing at how clever Joey was. She reached over and knocked his hat off, reminding him he wasn't the only smart one. When his hat fell to the floor, she noticed for the first time that he no longer had curly hair. Instead, his hair was so short that he almost looked bald. Looking at Joey, Teresa remembered how close she had come to cutting her hair.

"My first drill sergeant told me I would have to cut my hair if my bun kept coming loose. I was so glad when she found out that she was pregnant and got reassigned to a different unit."

Joey couldn't resist poking fun at Teresa. "Short hair might have looked worse on you than it does on me."

From their early days as wide-eyed children, Teresa and Joey had a strong desire to serve their community and positively impact the world around them. They always wanted a career that would enable them to extend a helping hand to those in need and protect the vulnerable. As they navigated the hallways of their high school, their aspirations became more defined, and they both shared the same dream of becoming police officers in the Air Force.

Their specialized police training consisted of hands-on training and classroom instruction. Teresa and Joe learned about military law and the rules for conducting investigations through written instructions. They got practical experience in self-defense, responding to emergencies, and rendering advanced first aid.

As a final run-through before graduation, each recruit was evaluated on their overall comprehension of the training through a mock scenario. The scenario allowed the police recruits to practice their judgment in a stressful situation while letting the other recruits learn by observing the simulated encounters.

Teresa and Joey were teamed up to run through an arrest scenario. Teresa was assigned the role of the police officer, and Joey played the suspect's part. The suspect had been driving recklessly and refused to pull over, so stop sticks were used to blow out the tires. The scenario begins with Teresa encountering Joey as he jumps out of his car.

In all the time Teresa and Joey had known each other, they had always been able to sort out any disagreements peacefully. Before joining the military, they talked about what might happen if they were pitted against each other in a performance evaluation as police officers. They decided to give it their all, putting in 110 percent. Their agreement showed that doing their job to the best of their ability was not about personal pride or taking things personally; it was about doing their job to the best of their abilities and supporting each other in the process.

After the drill sergeant said, "You both need to rise to the occasion," Joey started walking toward Teresa. Teresa directed Joey to stop, but he didn't. As soon as Joey got within five feet of Teresa, he lunged forward and swung, hoping to knock her down. Teresa quickly blocked his punch and tripped him. Before Joey had time to respond, Teresa had him rolled over and in a position to handcuff him with his arms behind his back.

The drill sergeant commended both of them.

"I was impressed that each of you understood the impact of your role. You have both proven yourself capable when facing significant physical and mental stress. Good job!"

Teresa and Joey were set to graduate from the police academy in two weeks. They needed to make a decision regarding their next duty assignment. Did they want to stay in the States, or did they want to go overseas? The best option came down to where they could be assigned together.

On the world stage, the tension between the United States and Iran was reaching a tipping point. Intelligence agencies were hearing a lot of chatter about drone attacks coming out of Iran, and satellite images showed enemy convoys moving closer to several American strongholds.

The Middle East Command began providing daily briefings to all the police recruits about the heightened danger and asked for volunteers to serve for one year in the region. Teresa and Joey raised their hands. They wanted to go where they could help the most.

Before their deployment to the Middle East, Teresa and Joey had to undergo additional combat training. They spent four weeks learning how to control convoy movements, capture and recover nuclear weapons, and various anti-terrorism responses. Their final qualifications for deployment to the Middle East were the grenade launcher and portable missile launcher.

After completing their rigorous training, Teresa and Joey emerged as two of the most highly skilled and confident police officers in the Air Force Security Forces. Their minds were sharp, their bodies were honed to perfection, and their hearts were filled with an unwavering commitment to serve and protect.

Teresa and Joey boarded a commercial aircraft for Germany that was full of tourists and German citizens returning home. They were the only passengers on the aircraft wearing battle dress uniforms. After landing in Germany, they transferred to a military cargo plane for entry into the Middle East.

As they descended onto the base in Iraq, they could see rows and rows of fighter jets and bombers on one side of the flight line. On the opposite side of the flight line, one- and two-story concrete buildings were arranged in alternating patterns. Rectangular sandbags made of burlap were stacked halfway up the sides of the buildings to provide added protection against shrapnel and small arms projectiles.

After disembarking the plane, they boarded a bus headed for the armory, where a sergeant escorted them into an underground vault. A few minutes later, a captain entered the room where they were waiting.

Sweeping his eyes over the room, he announced, "I have one thing to say. It's about weapons maintenance. Everyone will clean their gun before returning it to the armory."

Teresa and Joey were shocked when he turned around and walked out. The expectation was that he would talk about gun safety and checking guns out of the armory. Instead, they had gotten an unfriendly captain who didn't take any questions.

Iraq didn't look like or feel like anything in the States. Instead of spacious dormitories, soldiers were packed into small trailers, and the temperature often soared above 100 degrees Fahrenheit, sapping the soldiers' strength and blurring their vision. But the most challenging part was the constant noise—the generators running 24/7 to power the base and the jarring sounds of gunfire and explosions.

On their third day in Iraq, Joey and Teresa were assigned to ride together on patrols. They would meet outside the armory a few minutes before their shift started and pass the time with some good-natured teasing. Joey's nickname was Sasquatch because he was six inches taller than Teresa. Teresa's nickname was Grasshopper because she liked the color green. The banter would consist of them calling each other by their nicknames in an annoying tone. The teasing wasn't exciting to either one of them. Instead, it was a mundane routine that reminded them of their long friendship and provided a sense of normalcy to their chaotic day.

Three months after Joey and Teresa arrived in Iraq, the base threat level moved to the highest force protection condition. Ongoing talk about a likely missile attack on the base caused all the soldiers to be on high alert. Guard towers were staggered along the base perimeter. Bomb dogs patrolled around the aircraft twenty-four hours a day.

Intelligence specialists had gathered information about the movement of enemy forces in the local area. Teams began deploying into Baghdad, looking for any indicators of insurgents.

Joey and Teresa were a part of the second reconnaissance wave. Their team consisted of three Humvees, with five people in each vehicle. The front and rear vehicles had Browning machine guns mounted on top. The mount provided very limited protection for the person sticking their head out of the top of the Humvee. Their best protection was their Kevlar flak jacket and the gun in front of them.

As the team rolled into Baghdad, it felt like they were in a war-torn city from a movie. The devastation was too much for the mind to take in as real.

The driver in Joey and Teresa's Humvee pointed to a crumbling building. The walls still standing were riddled with bullet holes, and there wasn't any glass in the windows.

The driver said, "That was an apartment building at one time. Jerry used to get a kick out of stopping the convoy and giving candy bars to the kids. That was until he stepped on a booby trap that sent him home in a body bag."

Teresa and Joey's mission was uneventful, but the enemy's response to patrols in the area escalated over the next few weeks. They began to ambush patrols more frequently, and Teresa and Joey's squadron suffered increasing casualties.

The commanders of the patrols were faced with a difficult decision. They could continue to patrol the area, knowing that they were at risk of being ambushed, or they could withdraw from the site and risk losing control of it.

In the end, the commanders reacted by increasing the number of patrols. By ramping up their visible presence in the area, the military was sending a message to the enemy that they were ready and willing to defend their interests.

Two days after a patrol came under heavy fire, Teresa and Joey were on a morning reconnaissance mission to locate insurgents. They rolled out of the base's front gate at 4:30 in the morning. No one had anything to say in the early morning hours. Everyone was too busy thinking about the three marines killed by a suicide bomber just last week.

Teresa and Joey's team had orders to make a second sweep of a neighborhood where insurgents had been spotted a few days before. Their driver slowed down as he approached a main cross street in the area. Then, after looking around, he decided to turn right down a desolate street.

A group of four men became visible at the next four-way cross. They were in the street to the left. The street they were on had two vehicle lanes and a narrow sidewalk on one side. In front of one of the buildings, there were tables and chairs set up on the sidewalk.

The driver turned left and drove toward the men. The four men standing in the street became clearer to see, along with five more men sitting at different tables drinking tea as they got closer. Ten yards further down the street, a woman in a burka stood in the middle of the road. Her eyes were the only part of her face that was visible.

The men drinking tea stood up as soon as the second vehicle in the convoy turned on their street. They began to walk into the road, joining the other four men standing in the street. The men were lined up in single file, blocking the street, when the convoy reached them.

Teresa and Joey were in the first Humvee. Their driver flashed his headlights at the men standing in the street. They didn't respond. He rolled down his window and waved for them to move. They still didn't respond.

The driver waved again for the men to move. When they didn't respond, the driver radioed the vehicle behind them to back up. They couldn't move. Two men were standing in the street behind them.

The convoy commander radioed the order for the drivers to stay in the vehicles. The two policemen in the front and rear vehicles were to get out and fire a warning shot into the air.

After the four policemen fired their warning shot, the men in the rear of the convoy ran off, but the men standing in front of Joey and Teresa's vehicle started running toward them. The pre-op briefing stated to shoot anyone who failed to stop approaching after being warned. Teresa and Joey fired on the men, hitting two of the insurgents. After seeing two of their comrades lying in the street, the rest of the insurgents scrambled into an adjacent building.

Teresa and Joey jumped back into the Humvee. As the vehicle moved down the road, they saw the woman in the burka seated on the ground with her arms wrapped around a child. The child had been hiding behind the woman and was now lying in the woman's arms, soaked in blood.

When the vehicles slowed to render aid, firing from several buildings hit the front vehicle. The convoy commander ordered all vehicles to return to base.

Driving back to the base, Teresa felt detached from everything that was going on around her. It felt like she was watching herself in a movie. Joey felt overwhelmed and couldn't stop wiping the tears from his eyes.

Counselors were brought in—protocol after a civilian was hit. Once all the standard requirements were met, Teresa and Joey declined any further counseling. It was time to suck it up and move on.

Embracing the suck was the implied way to demonstrate confidence. It let the other military men and women know you had the physical and moral courage to handle whatever might happen.

The first test came in combat training when you proved you could hump a fifty-pound duffle bag on a ten-mile hike without complaints. But being physically strong wasn't enough.

Military men and women needed to know that everyone in their squadron was mentally strong. A soldier who wasn't strong enough to be self-reliant and handle their problems couldn't be trusted when it was time to go back out on patrol. You had to be able to walk the walk, swallow it, and move on.

Teresa and Joey spent five more months in Iraq. They continued to meet outside the armory before their shift started, but the playfulness stopped. They were exhausted after months of constantly being on guard against possible threats.

After being stationed in the Middle East for a year, Teresa and Joey got orders to go stateside. Teresa spent the next two years in California. Joey spent the remaining part of his enlistment in Illinois.

Before leaving Iraq, Joey and Teresa set a standing date. They promised to talk every year on the day they had to open fire. Combat had changed them.

Back in the States, Joey and Teresa kept up with each other through video calls and texts. They even talked about reenlisting together but decided against it. After their military time was up, they headed back home.

Joey had worked at his father's automotive parts store in high school, so he easily transitioned back to his old job. One day, as he was about to enter the store, a beautiful girl with green eyes and long brown hair walked up. Joey held the door open for her and asked if he could help her find anything. She was looking for windshield washer fluid, so Joey helped her find it and invited her to come back anytime she needed anything else for her car.

Two days later, the same girl returned to the store looking for an air freshener for her car. Joey learned her name was Jane.

Jane had returned to the store, hoping that Joey would ask her out. But after she realized her smile wasn't getting her anywhere, she decided to be coy.

Jane looked at Joey and said, "I'm never sure what I need for my car. I wish that I knew someone who could teach me about cars."

Joey saw through Jane's coy act. Without wasting any time, he asked her to go out for a movie and dinner that night.

Teresa didn't have a job to return to after her military time, so she applied for work as a security guard at the airport. Teresa took her responsibilities in the military very seriously, but after she started working at the airport she became obsessed with preventing any mishaps from happening.

One way for her to control the likelihood of an incident at the airport was to keep the traffic loop moving. Teresa was quick to motion a car to move on if it stopped for more than a few seconds, picking up or dropping off a passenger.

When things didn't go as planned, Teresa became unreasonable. An elderly lady made a complaint about Teresa being hostile toward her. Teresa threatened to arrest her if she didn't move her car, even though the lady saw her teenage grandson approaching the airport exit door with his luggage.

A few months after Teresa and Joey transitioned back into civilian life, their annual standing date rolled around. They decided to meet at the lake, which held fond memories for them.

Joey sat on the same picnic table he and Teresa had sat on at their high school graduation party, waiting on Teresa to arrive. He enjoyed feeling the warm sun on his face and reminiscing about his time with Teresa at the lake.

When Joey heard Teresa pull up in her car, he turned around and waved. When Teresa got close to the picnic table, Joey stood up.

After hugging each other, they took seats at the picnic table and looked out at the lake. The reflection on the water of the surrounding trees and bushes still appeared to be mysterious and magical. The lake looked the same, yet so much had changed.

As Joey reminisced about his past, he realized the last time he felt fully present in the moment was at the summer graduation party with Teresa. Innocence reigned supreme then, and he and Teresa were ready to conquer the world.

Joey asked, "Where did that old feeling go?"

Rather than trying to answer his question, Teresa opted to answer what she thought he was implying. "To be honest, I know that we set out to help. But now, I can't even help myself."

Feeling remorseful, Joey blinked back tears. "Jane has been hinting about making our relationship permanent. I don't deserve a family. I took a child away from another family."

Teresa had a flashback of the child who got shot, covered in blood. He had only been five or six. She stood up and started pacing in front of the picnic table. Then, in a deep guttural tone, she said, "We were savages, all there to kill each other. There had to be a different way."

Feeling unsettled, Joey reached down and adjusted his socks. "I know."

Teresa felt like someone had kicked her in the stomach. Remembering her fellow soldiers who were with her when the kid got hit, she said, "We had to open fire. We had to help find a way to get off that street."

Tears started to run down Joey's face. "Help is the worst four-letter word. I want to lock it down so it can't ever hurt us again."

Teresa was frozen in time, back on the street in Iraq. "I don't feel anything anymore. All I know is that things can go bad real fast."

The fly sitting on the picnic table listened to the conversation. It expressed Joey's guilt and Teresa's distrust of the world and everyone in it. The fly didn't know that Teresa and Joey accepted how they felt. They were damaged and profoundly changed.

Right now, being with each other was enough for Teresa and Joey. They didn't ask each other a thousand questions or tell each other how to feel. They knew that there weren't any answers for the burden they shared. But, as they looked out over the glistening water, they knew one thing.

They knew what they felt. They felt the love of a friend.

A GLASS ROSE

Staci and Madeline eagerly peered out from behind the bus stand, waiting for Juliet to arrive at the street corner. When they spotted Juliet looking around nervously, the two friends couldn't stop laughing. But as Juliet began to cross the street, they fell silent, holding their breath as they listened to the sound of her footsteps slowly getting closer.

When Juliet was just a few feet away, Staci and Madeline jumped out and, in menacing voices, said, "Nobody likes you!"

Juliet had encountered Staci and Madeline for the first time three weeks ago, at the start of the school year. She knew nothing about the girls and couldn't understand why they were being so mean to her at the bus stop.

After a week of being bullied every morning, Juliet tried leaving her house earlier to beat Staci and Madeline to the bus stop. But no matter how early she left home, Staci and Madeline were already there. She didn't know how they did it, but they were always waiting for her.

When Juliet confronted Staci and Madeline about saying cruel things to her, they just laughed. After a lot of thought, the only thing Juliet could conclude was that the girls were possibly testing her to see if she would report their behavior to the teacher. She realized that high school was quite different from middle school and that the "cool kids" didn't snitch on each other, so Juliet kept what was happening to herself.

Juliet did consider talking to her parents about what was happening at the bus stop but quickly decided against it. She didn't want her parents to go to the school and complain about Madeline and Staci. That could make things even worse for her. Besides, she was becoming an adult and needed to learn to handle things on her own.

Tattle-telling to the teacher had nothing to do with how Staci and Madeline treated Juliet. They were punishing Juliet for hanging out with Jack at the Friday night football games and sitting beside him at lunch.

Staci and Jack had been dating for six months until Jack called it off. Jack ended their relationship as soon as school started by telling Staci that it would be unfair to string her along while he was too young to think about getting serious.

Staci didn't believe Jack's explanation. She knew Jack was seeing someone else. That someone else was, apparently, Juliet.

Juliet had no idea about Staci's and Jack's breakup. She was simply trying to understand how to fit in during her first year of high school.

Everything came to a head when two girls walking by Juliet in the hallway gave her a dirty look and sneered the word "whore."

Juliet knew something had to change about how the other girls in school treated her, so she announced, "My name is Juliet. I would appreciate it if you called me by my name."

One of the girls knew how unforgiving the world was, especially regarding a girl's reputation, so she quickly replied, "Everyone knows that you walk around panty-less because you're a whore. Nobody wants to be friends with a skank like you. So enjoy your time with Jack because soon he'll realize how nasty you are and leave you too."

Staci and Madeline got what they wanted. After that, rumors started spreading like wildfire, and they were so scandalous everyone wanted them to be true.

Juliet couldn't believe how bad things had gotten. Just a month ago, she had been excited about starting high school and getting to pick her elective classes. She was going to figure out what she wanted to do with her life. Now, people saw her as some desperate girl who would do anything to be with a boy. Jack wasn't even her type; he was only a friend.

After talking to Jack, it became clearer why Staci and Madeline acted like they did. Jack and Staci's breakup didn't go well. Staci always had a better way for Jack to dress or act around other people. After growing tired of all the confrontations, Jack blamed the breakup on his not wanting to settle down. He knew that if he told Staci he didn't like her trying to change him, she would start crying and blame him for not understanding her.

Staci felt vindicated when Juliet's new nickname, *panty-less, stuck. Juliet's nickname came with so many* derogatory connotations that even her old friends from middle school started giving her the silent treatment. Juliet's only remaining friend was Jack, but they stopped eating lunch together after their class schedules changed.

After Juliet and Jack drifted apart, Juliet noticed that some girls liked to entertain each other at lunch by calling her by her nickname. The mean girls' loud voices and laughter made it impossible for Juliet to ignore them.

After a week of the mean girls' relentless targeting of her, Juliet started eating lunch alone in the library. She was much happier there. She could read a book or do her homework and didn't have to worry about being made fun of.

Another loner at school was Tony. No cruel whispers or targeted bullying followed him. He wasn't ostracized, not exactly. He was simply… an enigma.

A thunderous rumble followed Tony everywhere he went. His hair was the color of a storm cloud, and his eyes crackled like lightning, capable of earning him a detention slip with a single glance. His reputation as graffiti king and rumored owner of a pet snake named "Judgement" was a badge of honor in his twisted code of self-reliance.

Tony's fierce independence wasn't a choice; it was a fortress built of barbed wire, protecting a heart raw from the chaos of his home life. His mother, a whirlwind of tears and broken promises, and his father, lost in a haze of empty liquor bottles, had left him adrift in a sea of anger and hurt.

Tony and Juliet topped off the list of those whom people spread rumors about. That and Juliet's apparent lack of interest in other people, made Tony want to get to know her.

Tony decided to skip his first-period class just so that he could be waiting outside Juliet's classroom when the bell rang. As he waited for her class to end, he couldn't help but reminisce about the first time he saw Juliet in the hallway at school. She was simply stunning – with her long, flowing hair and big, beautiful brown eyes.

As soon as the bell rang, Juliet made her way out of the classroom. Her heart started pounding when she saw Tony standing there with a friendly smile, trying to say hello. She decided to ignore him, thinking this was just another cruel joke to mock her and call her by her notorious nick-name, "panty-less."

Tony's eyes lit up with excitement as he gazed at Juliet. "You know that we have our next class together. Maybe I could walk with you?" he said, his voice brimming with positivity.

Juliet hesitated for a moment, but Tony's sincerity soon won her over. "I guess that would be okay," she replied with a smile.

As Tony and Juliet walked side by side to their next class, they discovered their mutual interests in comics. Tony was thrilled to have found someone who shared his passion for comics, and Juliet enjoyed listening to Tony's stories about his collection. When Tony saw the door to the classroom, he stopped short. Juliet did, too.

"Would you like to go for a ride around the lake after school? I could take you home," Tony asked.

Juliet was tired of that depressing ride home on the school bus.

She hesitantly answered, "I imagine it might be fun. Why not?"

After school, it became a daily routine for Tony and Juliet to ride around the lake. Tony started teasing Juliet, saying, "I think you like me." Juliet was a bit hesitant to reveal her feelings, but eventually, she admitted that she always looked forward to seeing him. A few weeks later, Juliet and Tony became the new couple at school.

One day, while driving around the lake, Tony mentioned to Juliet that he knew a small group of people who were going to chill by the water on Saturday night. He invited Juliet to come along and suggested that they smoke a joint or snort meth together at the party. Despite having never tried drugs before, the red flags didn't come up for Juliet because she trusted Tony and believed he would never hurt her or ask her to do something that could spiral out of control.

On the night of the party, Tony went to pick Juliet up from her home. Juliet was having second thoughts about trying drugs. She was worried about losing control or doing something she would regret, but Tony was excited about trying something new together, and she didn't want to disappoint him.

Once they parked the car at the lake, Tony took a joint out of his shirt pocket and lit it. Juliet took a few hits and began to feel relaxed, but when she paused each time she wanted to say something, Tony realized they needed to get their energy up for the party.

Tony grabbed a plastic bag of white powder and a small tray from the glove box. He poured half a teaspoon of the powder onto the tray and handed it to Juliet. Tony stepped out of his car, looked around, and then took his driver's license and a twenty-dollar bill from his wallet before getting back inside the car.

Tony took the tray back. He used his driver's license to push the powder into two thin lines. He rolled the twenty-dollar bill into a straw. He took one end of the rolled-up bill and put it into one of his nostrils. He bent over and put the other end of the bill on the end of one of the lines of meth.

He took his index finger and pressed his free nostril down so no air could enter. He snorted and moved the bill up the line until it was gone.

He handed the rolled-up bill to Juliet and said, "The other line is for my girl."

Juliet felt a mixture of excitement and nervousness when Tony called her his girl, but most of all, she didn't want to disappoint him. Juliet took the rolled-up twenty-dollar bill and snorted her line.

A burning sensation began to fill Juliet's nose before she set the bill down. It reminded her of the time she got pool water in her nose, but the water had turned into fire this time. When her nose finally cooled off, an overwhelming feeling of happiness spread throughout her body.

Juliet had been to a party at the lake with Tony once before. That time, she felt uneasy and was constantly worried that someone might call her by her nickname, "panty-less." She knew that she had to be prepared to handle any hurtful teasing that might come her way, but in reality, she wasn't sure what to do.

Doing a line of meth changed everything for Juliet. She enjoyed talking to people she knew and people she had just met. Everyone seemed to feel the same towards her; they liked her and wanted to talk to her.

Juliet had a curfew of midnight, so Tony and Juliet decided to leave the lake around 11:00 p.m. to ensure she would make it home on time. As the car stopped in front of Juliet's house, Tony turned his head towards her, their gaze meeting in the moonlight. He leaned over and gently traced the curve of her cheek with his thumb, a feather-light touch that sent shivers dancing down her spine. Suddenly, everything around them faded away, and they became lost in each other, with only the feel of his lips on hers. As their kiss deepened, hands began to fumble with buttons and whispered pleas were drowned out by the pounding of their hearts.

As Tony walked Juliet to her front door, their laughter echoed through the quiet street, a testament to their growing connection. When

Tony leaned in to kiss Juliet goodnight, a silent conversation flickered between them, promising more moments to come.

Walking into her bedroom, Juliet noticed a straw basket filled with nail polish on her nightstand. She became fascinated with all the different names for pink and red polish as she took each bottle out of the basket. Juliet started lining up the polish from the darkest to the brightest across the top of her dresser. Before she knew it, she had spent four hours trying to decide if a few of the colors were darker or lighter than the ones next to them.

Even as the morning shone through Juliet's curtains, she still didn't feel sleepy enough to go to bed. She tried to watch her favorite TV show but found it difficult to concentrate. Determined to be productive, she tackled her upcoming week's homework but didn't get much done.

After not sleeping the night before and wasting most of the day, Juliet tried to nap later in the afternoon. She was exhausted, but all she did was toss and turn. She told herself that everything would return to normal tomorrow.

When she returned to her routine the following week, Juliet struggled to focus and found herself staring at the clock, waiting for the day to end. The only thing that made everything bearable was that Tony had gotten more meth for the upcoming weekend.

The following Saturday night, Tony and Juliet found a secluded spot to park the car at the lake. Tony got a small glass pipe and a half-full baggie from the car's center console. The pipe was a three-inch cylinder with a rounded end. Tony filled the bulb-shaped end of the pipe with the thin, small pieces of meth. Then, he took his lighter and started heating the bowl end of the pipe. Juliet was mesmerized as she watched what looked like shards of glass turn into a liquid. Tony waited until the meth cooled off and became solid again. After that, he held the lighter under the bowl until the meth started to smoke.

Tony said, "Watch this."

He inhaled the smoke. After he exhaled, he passed the pipe to Juliet. She relit the meth, watched it smoke, and inhaled.

A sudden rush of euphoria filled Juliet, along with an uncontrollable desire to tell Tony all about herself. Juliet talked about how since she had started high school, she always felt like she was being judged or treated like she was invisible, but when she did meth, she felt better about herself. Juliet wondered if being high at school would give her the self-confidence to stand up to all the mean girls.

Tony's unwritten rule about never doing drugs at school wasn't a badge of honor but a shield, a silent vow of self-preservation. He wasn't a saint, not by a long shot, but the threat of suspension and expulsion loomed over his every step.

Tony talked to Juliet about all the different punishments she might face if she got caught with meth at school, but Juliet was persistent. In the end, Tony reluctantly gave her enough meth for the next two weeks.

All of the negative feelings that Juliet had felt for too long vanished over the next week. She didn't feel her heart pounding or her armpits sweating whenever a girl looked at her in the hallway. The fact that her friends had deserted her because of a lie no longer bothered her.

Going into her second week, Juliet noticed she couldn't get back to the same rush of euphoria she had initially experienced. She increased the amount of meth that she snorted. The added lines helped some, but she couldn't return to the same feeling.

Over time, Tony became concerned about Juliet's meth use. She was talking about it all the time, and she kept needing more and more meth to get the same high. He suggested Juliet take a break from the meth or at least slow down.

Tony's reaction made Juliet suspicious. Maybe he didn't want her to feel confident. Wasn't that how some boys were—always trying to keep a girl insecure? She believed that one way or another, Tony was going to betray her.

When Tony and Juliet first started dating, Tony had been excited to see her, especially when they drove around the lake after school. But the once comforting melody of Juliet's voice, when he got her to admit she liked him, had morphed into a venomous hiss, each word dripping with accusations and threats when she didn't get all the meth she wanted.

Tony finally told Juliet: "You have to pick between me and the meth."

Juliet replied: "You don't get to control me. I'm better off without you."

Juliet went straight home after the argument with Tony. She ran into her bedroom and threw her jacket on the bed. Juliet sat on the chair beside her dresser and got the meth out of the drawer. She poured a line out on the top of the dresser, then got up to retrieve a dollar from her jacket pocket. When she stood up, she saw her reflection in the dresser mirror. Her eyes were sunken into her face, and scabs covered her arms.

The reflection of her skinny and scarred body in the mirror caused Juliet to pause. She could throw the meth out, get back with Tony, and start taking better care of herself. Or she could do the line of meth, feel good, and forget all the other stuff. Juliet rolled the dollar bill and snorted all the meth she had.

The next three days were excruciating. Juliet was in withdrawal and questioned if she had made the right decision to break up with Tony. She couldn't hold anything down; her body ached all over. Her thoughts cycled between "God, give me meth" and "God, never let me take meth again."

Juliet's parents pleaded with her to go to the doctor, but she convinced them she had caught a virus that was going around school. She would recover from the virus in no time; it was her breakup with Tony that was making her cry.

Juliet's parents understood that the end of a first romance could be a difficult and painful experience, especially for teenagers still learning about themselves. They decided not to interfere because they knew it was important for Juliet to feel independent and in control of her life. They gave Juliet cold medicine and soup and let her know they were there if she needed to talk.

Juliet finally emerged from her room, her eyes dull pools, reflecting the storm that had raged within her. She dragged herself back to school, but the teachers' words blurred, dissolving into a meaningless haze before they could solidify in her mind. Sentences became tangled threads, equations, a cryptic code she couldn't decipher.

When Juliet caught sight of Tony, she didn't feel angry. Instead, she experienced a sense of confusion and disconnection. It was as if she was looking through clouded glass, struggling to discern Tony's once-familiar features, which now seemed distorted and unclear. The bond they once shared, filled with joy and secrets, now felt broken and worn out.

Even when her old nemesis told her that Tony had moved on and left her behind, she didn't feel hurt. Her unsettling indifference to everything around her shocked her.

Juliet's days became a battle for motivation. Preparing for school was a daunting task as she lacked the energy to style her hair or choose an outfit. Even when her friends from the lake parties extended an invitation to join them for lunch, she couldn't find a reason to participate. Juliet realized she could stay in the dark abyss she called life or snort a line. Juliet switched back to "Give me meth; please let me find some more meth."

Now that Tony was no longer supplying Juliet with drugs, she needed money, so she started babysitting on Friday and Saturday nights. She always had work because she was always available, unlike the other teenage girls with friends to do things with on the weekend.

The money that Juliet made babysitting was enough to cover a twice-a-week habit. Juliet enjoyed the two days a week she had meth and could escape her depression, but the other days seemed unbearable.

Juliet needed more money, so she reached out to Lydia. Lydia held the third rung on the rumor ladder at school. Juliet held first place, and

Tony had second. The rumors about Lydia were that she would sleep with any guy if he paid her, and she didn't care who knew it.

At one of the lake parties, Lydia introduced Juliet to Mark, a student at the local college. Mark was cute in a nerdy way and had a couple of grams of meth in a bag in his jean pocket.

Mark started with small talk and quickly progressed to saying he wanted both of them to have a good time. Mark suggested they do a few lines now, and Juliet could take some home with her. The only stipulation was that Mark had a good time. If he did, Juliet could have a good time, too.

Lydia introduced Juliet to several other guys on the nights that Mark wasn't at the lake. One night, Juliet went with a guy who promised to share his meth with her. But, ultimately, he spat at her and told her he wouldn't pay for sex.

Everything had come full circle. Being called panty-less no longer fazed Juliet but waking up at three o'clock in the morning at the lake under a tree was terrifying. Nobody else was around, and the only sound was crickets chirping.

Luckily, there was a full moon. Juliet noticed her purse lying beside her and got her cell phone out of it. She called Lydia. There was no answer. She tried Mark. Still no answer.

The dark tree line beyond the lake made Juliet call home. She explained to her mother that Lydia had assumed she went home instead of spending the night at her house, so Lydia didn't look for her when she left the party. It was all her fault for falling asleep under the tree and causing the mix-up.

Juliet's explanation for falling asleep in the woods didn't convince her mom that Juliet was telling her the whole story. She had noticed some changes in Juliet—her acne had gotten worse, and she was losing weight—but Juliet's mom attributed these changes to Juliet's teenage hormones.

The next day, Juliet's mother was planning to punish her for being irresponsible, but when she saw Juliet curled up in bed and coughing, she decided to give her a few days to recover. She gave Juliet some cold medicine and told her to stay home from school until she felt better.

For the next three days, Juliet lay in bed tossing and turning, unable to get comfortable. Between passing out from exhaustion and waking up from the pain in her head, Juliet was hunched up in bed, throwing up in a trash can. She pleaded for the train to stop running through her head and for her body to stop shaking. But nothing she did could stop her from being dope sick.

On the fourth day, Juliet started feeling better physically, but she was upset with herself for not being able to remember everything that had happened in the last two weeks. In some ways, she wanted to know what she had done; in other ways, she hoped she never did.

One afternoon, while Juliet was recovering, she heard the doorbell ring. Her mother answered the door and invited Sarah inside. Sarah went straight up to Juliet's room. She knew exactly where to go. Juliet and Sarah had been best friends since elementary school.

Sarah knocked on Juliet's bedroom door. "Come in," Juliet called.

Sarah opened the door and stepped inside. Juliet was lying in bed, her book propped up on her knees. Juliet had heard the doorbell, but she wasn't interested. She enjoyed getting lost in her book, and she didn't like being disturbed.

Sarah threw her purse on the bean bag chair and walked over to Juliet's stuffed animal collection. She moved a few of the toys around until she found the clownfish.

Juliet sat up on the edge of her bed. She didn't feel like talking, but she felt like she had to say something.

"I...I remember that the clownfish was always your favorite," Juliet said.

Sarah asked, "Do you remember when we went fishing, hoping to catch a clownfish? Instead, all we caught were snapping turtles with the old bread and crackers we brought from home."

Remembering how fun that day had been made Juliet laugh out loud. Sarah had been a good friend then, but things were different now.

Suddenly apprehensive about Sarah's visit, Juliet snapped, "What made you come visit me?"

Hearing what she perceived as a frightened tone in Juliet's voice, Sarah tried to reassure her. "I was worried and wanted to make sure that you were okay. People at school said someone had attacked you and left you at the lake."

Feeling defensive, Juliet mocked Sarah. "Why all the concern now? We haven't talked in a while."

Sarah suddenly felt very immature compared to Juliet, so she turned away from Juliet and quietly said, "I've never been on a date. I've never even kissed a boy."

Juliet asked, "What does that have to do with your not talking to me?"

"I thought you didn't have time for me anymore," Sarah said. "I heard that you and Jack were a couple. Then you started dating Tony. I figured boys were the most important thing to you, so I left you alone."

Realizing that Sarah didn't have bad intentions, Juliet relaxed. "The rumors about Jack and me weren't true. We were just friends. Tony was my boyfriend, but everything got out of control."

"Why didn't you ever talk to me?" Sarah asked.

"A lot of the girls from our old school were calling me names," Juliet said. "They all seemed to turn on me, so I assumed you felt the same way."

Sarah said, "I knew all those girls talking about you were just jealous of you."

Sarah grabbed her purse, took a photo from her wallet, and handed it to Juliet. It was a photo of them in the fifth grade, smiling at the camera with their arms around each other's waists. Juliet's mom had taken the picture after they hung up a poster of their favorite rock band on Juliet's bedroom wall. They always planned to see the band in concert together when they were eighteen.

Looking at her friend, Juliet realized that the most painful part of the last few months had been trying to handle everything alone. She'd been so determined to prove that she wasn't a kid anymore that she forgot what a good friend Sarah was.

Walking to the bus stop on the first day after recovering from being dope-sick didn't look any different. Madeline and Staci were hiding behind the bus stand, waiting for her.

As soon as Juliet crossed the street, they jumped out and started walking toward her. They laughed and said, "Just wait."

At school, Juliet saw her name and phone number on the wall in the girl's bathroom stall with the legend, *druggie whore who puts out.* So she asked one of the girls, "Who wrote this?"

The girl answered, "I'm not going to talk to you. I don't want my name written all over the stalls in the boys' bathroom."

Mornings at the bus stop never changed. Writing on the bathroom walls didn't get erased. What had changed was that nothing and nobody would ever come between Sarah and Juliet again.

ON AGAIN, OFF AGAIN

The empty classroom came to life as Ms. Lombardi unlocked the door and flipped the switch. The fluorescent lights buzzed and flickered before finally illuminating the desks and the chalkboard at the front of the room. As she made her way to her desk, the sound of her shoes echoed throughout the silent classroom with a rhythmic tap-tap-tap on the linoleum floor.

After settling into her chair, she reached out and pressed the power button on her computer. The computer screen flickered at first, then brightened into a familiar desktop. As she scanned the array of icons on the screen, her eyes fell on the PowerPoint icon. She clicked on it, ready to start her workday.

Today's presentation on the potato famine in Ireland popped up. After checking the reader order for all the slides, Ms. Lombardi got the corresponding worksheets from the file cabinet and placed them on the students' desks. As a final preparation for the day, she set a bowl of potato chips on a table in the front of the classroom, hoping it would start the conversation about popular ways to eat potatoes today.

The last bell was about to ring, signaling the start of the school day, when Ms. Lombardi stepped into the hallway to check for any stragglers. As soon as the classroom door leading into the hallway closed behind her, Mike got up from his desk and started yelling, "Yo yo yo." All the other students stopped what they were doing and looked at Mike. He walked to the front of the classroom and grabbed a handful of the potato chips from the bowl, shoving them into his mouth. He kept this up until his cheeks started to bulge out.

Ms. Lombardi heard a lot of noise from the classroom while she was standing in the hallway. She took a deep breath and opened the door. As she entered the classroom, she quickly glanced around and noticed all the students were laughing at Mike. He was standing at the front of the classroom, trying to hide a smile. His cheeks were puffed out, and a pile of potato chip crumbs was on the floor.

Mike had always been a bit of a class clown, but he was also a good student and a kind person. He knew how to make people laugh without hurting anyone's feelings. So even though Ms. Lombardi usually didn't mind too much when Mike showed his mischievous side, she still had to call out his bad behavior.

Ms. Lombardi sternly said, "Mike, you need to get the broom out of the closet and clean up your mess. Then you can have a seat at your desk."

Mike's stomach churned as Ms. Lombardi's eyes met his. Her normally warm smile had vanished, replaced by a steely glint that sent a shiver down his spine. He knew his latest prank had crossed the line, but he liked how the other students' laughter made him feel connected to them, and he didn't want to give that up.

On occasion, Mike's behavior would become so distracting that it prevented the other students from focusing on their work. Ms. Lombardi's first form of discipline would be to take Mike's recess away from him. If that didn't work, Ms. Lombardi would schedule a conference with Mike's parents.

The most recent parent-teacher conference had to be rescheduled twice because of a conflict with Mike's father's schedule. Finally, a date was agreed upon, but his father canceled at the last minute. His mother attended the meeting and was eager to discuss his behavioral problems at school. She couldn't understand why Mike never misbehaved at home, yet he was so different at school.

Mike found himself sandwiched between his older brother, who was already ten, and his younger sister, who was only seven years old. Every evening, the family would eat dinner together at five o'clock. Right after dinner, the children would take their baths, and by seven o'clock, they would be in bed.

When Mike went to bed in the summer, the sun would linger in the sky until eight, sometimes even nine o'clock. Mike would lie in bed on the hot summer evenings, staring at the ceiling, listening to the other children outside playing. They would be laughing and chasing each other. It seemed unfair that he couldn't be out there with them.

On some evenings after dinner, Mike would ask his mother if he could stay up past his bedtime to play outside with the other children. Some days, his mom would let him play with the other children until 8 o'clock. On other days, she would yell at him for not understanding that she needed time for herself. Just his asking would cost him being able to watch TV for a week. He would have to go straight to his room after taking his bath while his brother and sister got to watch TV in the den for an hour.

Mike's family life was a series of precise routines and unwavering schedules. From the time they woke up to the time they went to sleep, every action was meticulously planned and executed with clocklike precision.

On occasion, Mike's parents would throw a curveball into the predictable rhythm of their lives. Instead of their usual Saturday routine of grocery shopping and yard work, they might surprise Mike by announcing a spontaneous trip to the zoo or a day at the beach.

Mike enjoyed the unexpected adventures, while at the same time, it was very confusing when his father announced that his soccer practice or his sister's t-ball practice got scratched off the schedule without any apparent reason. One day, Mike would be laughing; the next, he would be swept away by a storm he never saw coming. The uncertainty gnawed at him, a constant ache in his gut.

The summer before Mike entered high school, his parents gave him permission to throw a party in their finished basement. The main feature of the space was a contemporary L-shaped bar made of stainless steel and glass. On the top shelf of the bar, there was a collection of vintage heavy-cut crystal tumblers that Mike's father had discovered while browsing an antique store. These tumblers quickly became his most treasured possession.

Two days before the date, Mike's father told him that he couldn't have the party. He didn't trust Mike's friends not to trash the basement or break his prized bar glasses. Mike offered to move the bar glasses upstairs and clean up after his friends, but his father wouldn't change his mind.

Mike was furious at his father for waiting until the last minute to make him cancel the party. He had spent several weeks planning the party, inviting his friends, and building excitement around it.

Mike turned to his best friend, Adam, and vented about his frustration over late-night texts, using profanity and lamenting his "ruined" reputation. After Adam offered to host the party at his house, Mike called everyone invited and told them that the party had always been meant to be at Adam's.

Mike had always noticed inconsistencies in his parents' behavior, but he couldn't do much about it. However, when his father forced him to cancel his party, Mike's resentment towards his parents grew deep. He began to question the love and support they claimed to have for him.

After graduating high school, Mike finally felt he had the power to shape his own future. He no longer had to worry about the possibility of his parents unexpectedly changing their minds. This allowed him to make solid plans to pursue his dream of becoming a firefighter.

Once Mike completed his training at the fire academy, he was assigned to a fire station with a 24-hour on and 48-hour off-shift schedule. Mike and his fellow firefighters often went to each other's houses and played cards on their days off. At one of these gatherings, Mike met his wife, Janet.

Mike and Janet welcomed their son Danny into the world a year after their wedding. As their son grew, new challenges emerged, but they remained steadfast in their commitment to each other.

Mike and Janet loved to spend their leisure time together. They would often take impromptu road trips, listening to old rock and roll tunes and stopping at peculiar roadside attractions. On one occasion, they purchased homemade jams from a sun-wrinkled farmer under a crooked apple tree in a small town. In another town, they shared stories with a witty waitress about tales of UFO sightings. As they made their way back home, they would hold hands and run their thumbs over the grooves of their wedding rings, silently communicating their deep connection and trust in each other.

One afternoon, the klaxon shrieked through the quiet stillness as Mike shot through the firehouse doors. The call crackled through the speaker – "Apartment fire, multiple floors, possible trapped occupants."

The sound of firefighters fastening buckles, the exchange of urgent instructions, and the sudden roar of the fire engine filled the air in mere seconds. As the firefighters raced towards the fire, images of terrified faces peering from windows flashed in Mike's mind while the gut-wrenching cry of a child lost in the smoke echoed in his mind.

Mike tightened his helmet strap and secured his oxygen mask before charging into the burning building. He was immersed in a raging inferno, flames whirling around him, their intense heat searing through his fireproof suit. Mike narrowed his eyes against the stinging smoke as he stumbled upon a woman huddled in a corner, eyes wide with terror. Without a word, he hoisted her onto his broad back and retraced his steps through the smoke-choked building.

For Mike, this was just another day. Another fire was fought, and another life was saved, but his heroism impressed management. They saw that he had the potential to be a great leader, and they offered him a promotion to lieutenant.

Mike was committed to having the division's best firefighting and rescue unit. He would schedule five real-life scenarios each day to improve his crew's skills. Before passing out the activity log, Mike would designate one person to lead each activity. However, during the activity, Mike would often step in and assume control from the person he had put in charge.

Mike was aware that his fellow firefighters were not happy about being treated as though they were untrustworthy to act or make a decision on their own. Mike did not necessarily doubt their abilities. He was about 99 percent confident that his crew would make the right call when faced with whether to fight a fire or evacuate a building. However, in the back of Mike's mind, he wondered if anyone could ever really know someone else. Even his parents were difficult to comprehend, often saying one thing and then suddenly doing something else.

A simmering tension emerged between Mike and Janet after Mike got promoted. Mike seemed distracted by work, so Janet asked him how he felt. When Mike said everything was fine, Janet kept pushing. Mike felt like Janet was trying to turn their differences into a competition, where if Mike talked to her, then she was happy, and if not, then he was happy.

Mike contemplated using his secret weapon, humor, to appease Janet. Since elementary school, making other people laugh had been Mike's way of hiding his inability to understand people. But the problem was that he didn't find Janet's being upset with him amusing, so he started creating projects around the house. His days became consumed with a flurry of activity, leaving little time for meaningful conversation with Janet.

When Janet realized that Mike was intentionally trying to avoid her, she decided to try a different way to connect with him. She would bring Mike a glass of water while he was working on a project, hoping they would have the opportunity to talk when he took a break. But Mike would quickly gulp his water down and go back to work.

Once Mike saw that the options for avoiding talking to Janet were wearing thin, he decided to remodel the spare bathroom. He tore out the bathtub, the commode, and the sink. If Janet wanted to talk, he would tell her he had to run to the hardware store. They could talk later. He felt like a child making excuses, but he couldn't stop.

After continuously trying but still not getting the response or reaction from Mike that she wanted, Janet decided things had to change. She knew that Mike was preoccupied with something, and she wanted to know what it was. The breaking point was when she asked Mike if he was having an affair.

Mike was shocked that Janet would question his fidelity. Not only had he never cheated on his wife, he had never even been tempted. The whole idea seemed so ridiculous to him that he wondered if Janet was trying to push his buttons, heighten the drama as a way to force him to talk.

As days turned into weeks, the chasm between them began to eat away at Janet. She announced to Mike that there would also be a physical separation since he was so emotionally distant. They would be sleeping in separate beds. Janet's ultimatum made Mike feel rejected and alone, like when he was a child going to sleep in the daylight while everyone else had fun.

The re-emergence of childhood memories pushed Mike into self-protect mode. The last thing Mike wanted was to have separate bedrooms, which could lead to different houses and a divorce, but he had learned as a child that he could really only rely on himself, so now he would take care of himself again.

After a week of sleeping in the spare bedroom, Mike stopped thinking about how he would face the worst if it happened and started wondering why he thought it might happen. He decided to be sensible and talk to Janet about how he was feeling.

When Mike came home from work the next day, he found Janet sitting on the couch reading a book. He went over to her and sat down next to her. Mike put his arms around her and held her close. He didn't want to let go. He wanted to stay there forever, just holding her in his arms.

When Janet pulled away and looked up at him, Mike said, "It's been hard sleeping away from you, Janet. You have been a part of everything good in my life. I am so grateful that you are my wife."

Not having Mike in bed with her had made Janet think of their bedroom as the loneliest place in the world. She had decorated it just the way she wanted, and the bed was big and comfortable, but without Mike, what was it worth?

With relief, she said, "I love you too. I don't want you to think I'm trying to make you pay some price for being distant. I've missed you and the connection that we used to have."

Mike felt guilty for the way that he had treated Janet. The memory of running off to the hardware store stabbed him.

Mike's voice was barely a whisper as he said, "It's all my fault. The walls I built around myself have kept me from being honest with you."

As Janet sat opposite Mike on the couch, her eyes held a mixture of gratitude and relief, and a soft smile played on her lips.

"Thank you," she said, her voice soft but steady. "It means a lot to me that you share how you feel."

Mike admitted, his voice rough. "Seeing you unhappy... it tore me apart. I couldn't bear it any longer."

Mike paused, gathering his thoughts. "It all goes back to..." He hesitated, then continued, "It all goes back to my having to take care of myself from a very young age. My mom was always preoccupied with having time to herself, and my dad cared more about material things than anything or anybody else. I might be able to understand all of that, but the part I never got was how they could be so contradictory. One day, they wanted to spend time with us kids, but the next day, they didn't want anything to do with us."

"That had to be very confusing."

Sitting on the edge of the couch, Mike could feel his fists clenching, his face burning with a mixture of anger and sadness. The words tumbled out of his mouth, a torrent of emotions he had kept bottled up for far too long.

"My parents taught me not to listen to what they said but to wait and see how they acted. So, I grew up with a lot of doubt about whether I could trust people."

Suddenly, Mike remembered those nights he would ask to play outside. Just ask—not actually sneak out or break any rules.

Janet reached over and put her hand on Mike's arm. "There's nothing wrong with you— not more than any of the rest of us. Your parents hurt you, and you were trying to protect yourself from being hurt again."

"It's always been hard for me to talk about how I feel," Mike said. "It always feels like one of those doors, you know, where you don't know if it's a lady or a tiger behind it."

Mike chuckled. "I don't ever want to disappoint you."

Janet smiled, her heart lighter.

She looked Mike in the eye and said, "That will never happen. You're perfect to me."

The following morning at work, Mike felt like he had turned a corner. After he assigned the activity schedule to his crew of firefighters, they started blaming each other for how the training had gone wrong last week. Rather than giving in to his old nagging feeling to step in and take control, Mike told them they needed to work together to figure it out.

After finishing his day at work, Mike grabbed his car keys from his desk and headed home. It had been a long day, but he was feeling good.

Mike parked his car in the driveway and walked up to the house. As he opened the front door, he heard his son, Danny, running down the hall to meet him. Danny was shouting, "Daddy, Daddy." Danny jumped into his arms as soon as he crossed the door's threshold.

The sensation of his son hugging him around the neck reminded Mike of how lucky he was to have a family separate from his parents. With gentle but firm hands, he placed his palms on Danny's shoulders and gradually pried him away so he could see into his eyes. Mike smiled at him and kissed him on his forehead.

Mike carried Danny into the kitchen. Janet was chopping up vegetables for a salad. He walked over to her, and with their son in between them, he hugged her. Mike was so grateful for Janet. He finally felt safe, trusting that he could count on another person.

RED FLAG

The sensation of moving forward was very odd. Brandon imagined that, to an observer, he might look like he was flying, but he felt like his body was falling, like going down in an elevator. An overwhelming sense of dread filled Brandon as he was pulled along different streets. He tried looking into the windows of the buildings as he went past them, but he was going too fast. He felt relieved as he circled back toward the corner grocery store where he liked buying comic books. Then, just before he made what he thought was the last turn, he felt his father's hand squeezing his face. His father was shaking his head from side to side, yelling at him to wake up so he could deliver the morning papers.

Brandon jumped out of bed as his dad walked out of his bedroom. He quickly got dressed and grabbed his cart to haul the newspapers.

Brandon stepped out into the frosty morning, his breath billowing out in white puffs that quickly vanished in the frigid air. He glanced down at the porch, where a neat stack of newspapers sat waiting, their dark rectangles stark against the snow. With practiced ease, he tossed them onto the metal cart beside him, the added weight making the handles dip slightly.

With each step, a newspaper sailed through the air, landing with a soft thud on snowy lawns. Despite wearing his warmest boots and two pairs of socks, Brandon's toes were curled tight like tiny, chilled fists. He tried everything to warm them up—stomping his feet, hopping on one foot and then the other, but nothing worked. After he realized that all his attempts to stay warm were futile, he began flinging newspapers toward houses with a careless flick of his wrist. It wasn't just the cold urging him forward; he had to make it back in time to walk with his younger brother and sister to school.

When Brandon got home, he found his brother and sister sitting at the breakfast table, finishing their oatmeal. His mom immediately started rushing him to hurry up and eat. She handed him an envelope containing the monthly tuition when he finished eating. Brandon would drop the dues in the box outside Sister Mary's office before attending his first class.

Brandon tugged on his oversized 4th-grade uniform as he walked through the front door of Saint Francis Catholic School. He saw Mr. Caprice standing by the water fountain, jabbing his index finger into Larry's chest. He wanted to make sure that Larry understood that saying the Lord's name in vain was a quick pass to burn in hell.

Larry and Brandon gave each other a nod. They knew that Mr. Caprice's shoes had holes in the bottoms, but this year, theirs didn't.

As the school day began, a gentle chime accompanied the first rays of sunshine that peeked through the classroom windows. Brandon was no stranger to the usual routine of reciting prayers, singing hymns, and studying multiplication tables, but today was Friday. He was looking forward to the weekend, the sweet promise of freedom from periodic tables and catechism lessons.

Walking through the front door after school, the familiar scent of lemon furniture polish hit Brandon and his siblings like a wave. Without exchanging any words, they tiptoed through the house to their bedrooms.

Just like always, their beds were made, and the pillows were fluffed. There were no clothes on the floor, no books on the nightstands, and no personal belongings anywhere to be seen. They put their backpacks and coats in their bedroom closets and headed to the kitchen for a snack.

Brandon went to the cabinet and took out a box of crackers and a jar of peanut butter. After he poured three glasses of milk, Brandon sat down at the table with his brother and sister to enjoy their snacks.

After they finished their snack, Brandon picked up the three empty glasses and took them to the sink. Turning on the water, he rinsed them off and put them in the drying rack. After wiping down the table, he went outside to join his brother and sister in the backyard for an hour before starting his homework.

While listening to Brandon and his siblings playing outside, Brandon's mom started looking around the house to see if the children had messed anything up without noticing. Walking past the bathroom, Brandon's mom noticed a mark on the door where someone had pushed it open with their shoe. Reaching under the bathroom sink, she took out a bottle of spray cleaner and a sponge. She sprayed the cleaner on the door and noticed her hands shaking. She tried to calm herself down, but it was no use. She was still upset from the night before.

Realizing time was running out, she took a deep breath and let it out slowly. She put the final wipe on the door and went into the kitchen to finish dinner. The pot roast was in the oven, the potatoes were ready to be mashed, and the peas were in the pot when the car pulled into the driveway.

As the back door closed, the first thing to be heard was an angry exhale. It almost sounded like a person was clearing their throat. The next sound was Brandon's father's feet stomping on the floor as he walked toward the kitchen.

Brandon's mom started looking for the potato masher. As she moved the utensils around in the drawer, she hoped that her rattling around in the kitchen would make her husband focus on his hunger rather than finding a reason to get angry.

Brandon's father entered the kitchen and stopped beside his wife. He breathed heavily even though the distance from the back door to the kitchen wasn't long. Then, without warning, he balled up his fist and hit the counter.

Brandon's mom jumped as his dad leaned in close enough for her to feel his breath on her face.

He demanded, "What have you been doing all day?"

Brandon's mom wanted to run out of the kitchen, but she knew her husband would follow her, and then, he would only be madder.

In a meek voice, she answered, "Taking care of the children and cleaning up the house."

Brandon's mom closed the utensil drawer and stirred the peas on the stove. She had intentionally turned her back on her husband so he couldn't see her lips quivering.

When his father got home, Brandon was hunched over his desk, grappling with a math problem. The crisp white pages of math worksheets were spilling out of his backpack onto the floor. But after Brandon heard the kitchen door slam shut, he couldn't concentrate on his homework anymore.

Even through the closed kitchen door, the shouting made it easy for Brandon to hear what his parents were saying. His dad demanded to know who had pushed the screen out of the door, and his mom kept saying she didn't know. The next thing Brandon heard was a slapping sound and Mom crying.

After Brandon heard the kitchen door open, he felt an overwhelming fear creeping into his body, slowly paralyzing him from the inside out. His heart pounded as he listened to his father's footsteps coming down the hallway toward his bedroom. When Brandon heard his father walk past his bedroom door, he was about to breathe a sigh of relief, but suddenly, the door was pushed open, and his father came into the room.

Brandon's father didn't ever explain his angry outbursts to anyone in the family and had never said anything to Brandon even remotely similar to, "Bend over my knee so I can spank you." Instead, his belt went flying and hit wherever it happened to land.

After his father left, Brandon slipped off the back of his bed and ran outside. He kept out of sight while his father cooled off by sitting in the backyard with his back against the house. Eventually, he would hear the TV playing in the living room as dishes rattled around in the kitchen. Dinner was on the table every night at six o'clock, regardless of anything else.

Tonight, Brandon was eating his roast beef and mashed potatoes while his dad kept his eyes on his plate, and his mom tried to smooth things over by asking if anyone wanted something else to eat. His brother and sister were bickering. It was always the same thing. They would argue about whose turn it was to load the dishwasher.

While Brandon was aware of everything happening at the dinner table, he was especially attuned to his father. He could detect the subtle shifts in his father's mood, the tightening of his jaw, the clenching of his fists, long before anyone else. When the warning signs appeared, Brandon would try anything to distract his father, to appease him, or to divert his anger away from his mother and siblings. He would tell him stories, sing him songs, and make him laugh. Sometimes it worked, sometimes it didn't. But Brandon's mom and his siblings always laughed at his humor and stories because everyone in the family, including his father, expected Brandon to be the one to calm the storm.

A few weeks later, one of the nuns from school called Brandon's mom about a fight that broke out when the boys were playing baseball. Trying to hit the ball thrown by the pitcher, one of the boys swung the bat, which flew out of his hand and hit Brandon in the leg.

Brandon learned from his father that if you were angry, you should hit someone. He learned that if you were frustrated, you should hit someone. So, when the boy swung the bat, and it hit him in the leg, Brandon reacted instinctively. He punched the boy and knocked him to the ground.

When Brandon's father got home, he heard about the fight from his wife. She told him the other boy had started it, but the school still called, threatening to suspend Brandon the next time he got caught fighting.

Brandon tried explaining the fight to his father, but he wasn't interested. All that mattered to him was that he was wasting his money paying for a Catholic school that Brandon might get kicked out of.

When Brandon insisted that the other kid throwing the bat started the fight, he heard his father sucking his breath across his teeth. Suddenly, his father threw his arm and hit Brandon across the face with the back of his hand. The blow was hard enough to cause Brandon to knock over the side table as he fell backward.

When Brandon entered high school, he found himself seeking refuge outside the walls of his home. In school, he discovered a world of opportunities where he could be free from the toxic presence of his abusive father.

Brandon found a haven in the lively and enthusiastic atmosphere of the debate team. After years of feeling ignored, finally he felt acknowledged and heard during brainstorming sessions. Brandon savored the camaraderie, the genuine smiles, a warmth he rarely felt at home.

Brandon appreciated the bond he had formed with other members of the team, but he couldn't decide what people would think if they knew he got knocked around at home. Would they see it the same way as he did? His father was a bully who only picked on people who couldn't defend themselves. Or would they see him lacking something other people had? Would they blame him?

Brandon built a fortress around himself, a facade of normalcy that concealed the turmoil within. He plastered a smile on his face, a mask that hid the anger at his father simmering beneath the surface. Brandon laughed at jokes he didn't find funny and echoed opinions he didn't share. But behind the mask, the shame whispered insidious lies in his ear, telling him he was worthless, undeserving of love, a stain on the fabric of society.

One way Brandon tried to blend in was to wear a collared shirt on Fridays, just like the other guys on the debate team. But if the shirt Brandon got out of his closet that morning didn't lie like he thought it should, he would start sweating, and his heart rate would go up. Sometimes, the churning in his stomach would make him run into the bathroom and throw up. When Brandon would return to his bedroom, he would throw the shirt on the floor and grab a t-shirt from his dresser drawer to wear that day.

On an intellectual level, Brandon knew that his anxiety about a shirt was irrational and exaggerated, but that didn't stop him from feeling overwhelmed. Brandon believed his inability to control his mind was a sign that he might never be good enough or genuinely belong.

After leaving home, Brandon's hard-learned persuasion skills easily translated into a thriving consulting career. Early on, Brandon had assumed the responsibility of keeping his mom and siblings safe while things were falling apart around them. He was the one whom everyone in the family expected to persuade his father to choose not to be angry or become violent.

Brandon's consultant job came with a unique set of challenges and rewards. The long hours were demanding, and the clients could be difficult, but Brandon enjoyed traveling to unusual places. He would fly to the client's site on Monday mornings and return home on Thursday nights.

While packing his clothes for the trip, Brandon didn't want to risk feeling like he did in high school when just looking at a shirt that didn't fit could make him run to the bathroom to throw up. So he had the dry cleaners fold his dress shirts and put them in a plastic bag just like they were new shirts from the store.

On the flight to meet his new client, Brandon would cycle through all the possible things that could go wrong. He would worry about saying the wrong thing, losing control, or being judged as incompetent.

All the what-ifs would make Brandon feel anxious, but once he started working with the client, he would come off as confident and ready to troubleshoot any problems that might come up. Brandon would shift his what-if list into a to-do list.

After spending all day with his client, Brandon would relax at his hotel. He'd shower, use one of his apps to have food delivered, and turn on the TV.

Brandon would gaze at the TV screen while he thought about his day. He frequently found himself fixating on every little detail of his day, replaying conversations in his mind and searching for any errors he may have made. Some nights, the only way Brandon could prevent his thoughts from spiraling out of control was to listen to himself talk through his feelings out loud.

Brandon often found himself lying in the hotel bed, his eyes closed and unable to rest. He would toss and turn in the bed, the day's events looping through his mind like a broken record. After a while, Brandon would start to feel desperate, worrying about what might happen if he didn't get any rest. What if the client notices I'm not as sharp as I used to be? What if I forget something? What if I'm impatient with the client?

Brandon's overthinking was a habit, a voice in his head that never stopped questioning, analyzing, and criticizing, but he didn't know how to break it. All the what-ifs only ended with him being constantly exhausted and more anxious.

One Friday afternoon, Brandon and another consultant, Adam, were in the office finishing their reports for that week's site visits. Brandon decided to see if Adam was interested in discussing the uneasy feelings that he had been having.

"These site visits involve a lot of stress," Brandon said.

Adam sighed and said, "There's a lot of preplanning involved, and you never know if you will end up with a nightmare client. My last client changed the plan halfway into the visit, even though all the expectations were agreed upon weeks prior. Switching things up at the last minute makes everybody uncomfortable."

Listening to Adam vent his frustrations made Brandon believe they shared a similar perspective. Feeling reassured, he decided to confide in Adam about some of the things he had kept bottled up inside.

"One time, I thought I was having a heart attack after dealing with one of those idiot clients. I almost went to the emergency room, but then, after a few minutes, my heart stopped racing, and I felt like I could breathe. I realized it wasn't a heart attack, just my anxiety."

While listening to Brandon talk, Adam remembered that thinking differently about situations helped him push through hard times in his own life.

Trying to help, Adam replied, "You always look so cool, calm, and collected. But, look, I get nervous sometimes when I have to tell a client I can't do something. I tell myself that everyone feels nervous sometimes. It's not a big deal. It passes after I move on to the next part of the assessment. Think positive. Don't make a problem where there isn't one."

Adam knows how to handle things, Brandon thought. *He can calm himself down.*

Anger flared within Brandon, hot and prickly, directed at himself and his seemingly insatiable need to control the future. He was tired of being cursed with his need for perfection, always left feeling isolated and misunderstood.

Brandon was determined to prove to himself and everyone else that he could be just like them. So, he poured his heart and soul into creating the perfect way to control his anxiety. He meticulously crafted an exercise program and a bedtime routine and was determined to follow them with unwavering resolve.

His exercise regimen became a rigid ritual, a duty he performed even when exhaustion weighed him down. He pushed past fatigue, ignoring the nagging pain in his muscles, driven by an almost compulsive need to adhere to his self-imposed schedule.

His sleep routine was equally rigid. He retreated to his bedroom at precisely the same time each night, regardless of his actual fatigue. The once-relaxing rituals became monotonous, the darkness of his room feeling more like a prison than a sanctuary.

Brandon's pursuit to control his anxiety quickly reached a breaking point. He realized that his trying to control everything was the very thing that was controlling him.

At one of his site visits, Karen, the section chief, could not grasp the need to change how she had been doing something for the past two years. Brandon tried explaining it many different ways, but she wouldn't budge.

When Karen threatened to go over Brandon's head because she disagreed with his findings, Brandon felt his breath quicken, his palms becoming slick with sweat. Karen's ultimatum made Brandon feel the same way he did when his father let him know he had control over him.

Brandon refused to let Karen's threat cause him to doubt his decision, so he stormed into her office and exclaimed, "If you don't listen to my suggestions, then you will fail the upcoming inspection."

Then, Brandon drove his message home by saying, "I'm tired of trying to fix everyone."

The shocked look on Karen's face made Brandon realize he had crossed the line. Brandon immediately told her that he was having a bad day and apologized. But, even after she said she understood, Brandon knew that some people he worked with would never get their life together. Still, he couldn't get his life together, either.

Later that night, Brandon woke up in the hotel room bed thinking about how early in the day, while interacting with Karen, his heart had started pounding, and his stomach churning. He remembered feeling that same way as a kid when his father crept closer with a belt in his hand.

Brandon got out of bed and went into the bathroom. He splashed some water on his face and looked at himself in the mirror. He looked tired, but he also looked determined.

With his mind made up, he walked back into the room. He sat at the desk and opened his laptop, searching for therapists near his house. He found a few that looked promising, and he made an appointment with the first one he could get in to see.

On the morning of his appointment, Brandon's mind was racing. He contemplated calling the therapist's office and canceling, but then he moved on to thinking that he could always use a meeting at work as an excuse to cut the appointment short if he found the therapist wasn't a good fit for him.

Later that day, Brandon sat in the therapist's waiting room, questioning the decision he had made earlier that morning. His heart was pounding so hard that he could feel it in his throat. He bent over in his chair and put his head in his hands, trying to calm himself down.

Brandon looked up when he heard the door to the therapist's office open. A woman in her early forties with long brown hair and a warm smile stepped out.

"Brandon?" she asked.

After Brandon nodded yes, the therapist said, "It's nice to meet you."

Brandon stood up and shook her hand. "It's nice to meet you, too," he said.

The therapist led Brandon into her office and gestured for him to sit down. "So," she said, "Why don't you tell me what brought you into the office today?"

The anxiety that Brandon had noticed when he first walked into the office intensified. But so did something else, an elusive feeling.

Eager to know if he had made a mistake, Brandon decided not to waste anyone's time.

He jumped right in. "I get stuck in these loops of endless thoughts. It's like I overanalyze everything."

Wanting to show Brandon that she understood what he was saying, the therapist replied, "That sounds exhausting. Sometimes, we overanalyze things because we're responding with our backdrop. Our backdrop is everything about us and the entirety of our life experiences. Our backdrop affects how we react to things that happen to us every day."

Not being accused of blowing things out of proportion or being told to question himself was a relief for Brandon.

Exhaling, he said, "I spend so much time thinking about how things could go wrong or not according to my plan. I feel like I'm never happy, no matter what the situation is."

"What do you mean, never happy?"

Brandon paused, unsure what reaction he could expect when answering the question. But when he considered all the energy he put into worrying and agonizing over the past and the future, Brandon knew he could withstand any response the therapist threw at him.

"I don't like myself," Brandon said with a frankness that startled him. "I let my worry control how I spend my time. I look at all the successful people; they aren't persistently paralyzed like me. I should be able to do better."

"It sounds like you have a voice in your head that likes to point out your flaws and mistakes."

Brandon turned away from the therapist, looking out the window as if searching for something, then said, "You don't want to know how I talk to myself. I wouldn't say some of the things I say to myself to my worst enemy."

"Storytelling is a tool I use with clients to help them bypass their go-to of over-analysis and take them straight to their feelings. Can I tell you a story?"

Brandon answered: "Sure."

The therapist smiled, a crescent-shaped smile reaching the corners of the eyes, just before she said, "Imagine that you are in an airplane. The airplane experiences engine trouble and suddenly takes a nosedive toward the ocean. What kind of response do you think you would have?"

Brandon quickly answered, "My heart would be racing, and I would be scared, wondering if the plane was going to crash."

The therapist nodded her head in agreement and continued.

"Not knowing how someone might react or not knowing what might be around the corner can instill the same feeling in people with anxiety as being in a plane crashing into the ocean. A person with anxiety can feel this level of worry over anything unknown. It can be anything from an upcoming exam at school to a serious medical diagnosis."

Weary from all his attempts to understand his anxiety, Brandon suddenly felt relief.

"That's it. I feel my anxiety in my body and my mind."

"You are almost there," the therapist said.

Brandon interjected, "Sometimes I don't have any control over my feelings. I get trapped in a vicious cycle and don't know how to turn my mind off."

Understanding how overwhelming it was to deal with anxiety, the therapist said, "I'm here to help you understand why you can't turn off your feelings."

"Where do I find the answer?"

Knowing that a single question has many different answers, the therapist replied, "Millions of people feel the same way you do. Some people come to understand what brought them to where they are by talking about their feelings and experiences. Others may need medications to help them feel calmer before they are ready to talk to their therapist. That's something you and I will need to figure out together."

Feeling at a loss for words, Brandon nodded his head in agreement.

Not wanting to sound vague, the therapist decided to use another story. "One client of mine grew up with an abusive father. When she got older, she tried to control everything in her life because she never wanted to feel out of control like she did when her father had power over her. But, she found trying to control everything caused her a lot of anxiety. She was one of my clients who needed medication before she felt comfortable talking to me because her memories about her father were so traumatic."

"I could understand that," Brandon said.

As a way to pull together everything they had discussed, the therapist said, "What I'm getting at is that there are many reasons for anxiety. So the first step is to control your uncomfortable feelings and then figure out what is causing those feelings."

Brandon took a moment to consider everything that they had talked about.

He hesitantly admitted, "I've been struggling for as long as I can remember. I need some help to figure this out."

"While the past might have brought you here, what matters most is that you're taking charge of your own future," the therapist said. "By coming here, you've opened the door to change and improvement, and that's something to celebrate."

Brandon was glad that his anxiety hadn't been able to convince him to cancel this appointment.

With a sigh of relief, he said, "I underestimated the significance of finding someone who understands what it's like to walk in my shoes. I want you to know that I appreciate you."

Wanting to give Brandon something he could use the next time he felt the grip of anxiety, the therapist decided to share a method that worked for her.

"One trick I use when I feel anxious is mindful breathing. I breathe in through the nose until my stomach expands, and then I slowly let the breath out through my mouth. It doesn't always calm me, but it lets me focus on the here and now."

Listening to his therapist talk gave Brandon a sense of calm that he had never felt before. He wasn't thinking about the past or the future; he was in the moment.

The therapist interrupted Brandon's curious thoughts by asking, "See you at the same time next week?"

Brandon was tired of living inside his head, so he answered, "Yes, you will."

Now Brandon knew what that elusive feeling had been: Hope.

IT TAKES TWO

Tina and Bob had never been formally introduced, but they would often pass each other on the sidewalk on their way to class. They would always smile and nod at each other. It was a simple gesture, but it was a way of saying that they were happy to see each other, even if it was just for a moment.

Tina told her friends about the cute guy she would pass on the sidewalk, and they were all very excited for her. They had never seen Tina so happy before, and they wanted to know everything about him.

When Tina told her best friend, Sarah, that she knew nothing about him, Sarah became a bit skeptical. She worried that Tina might get involved with someone she might later regret.

Sarah decided to do some snooping. She talked to some of her friends in the same classes as Bob. After discovering his full name, she looked him up on social media and read some of his old posts.

Sarah's snooping didn't turn up anything bad, but she did find out that Bob was in his final year of graduate school, just like Tina and herself. He was single, and he had told some of his friends that he was interested in Tina.

The following Saturday morning, Bob was doing his laundry at the laundromat when he saw Tina sitting in a chair, scrolling on her phone. He was so excited to see her that he almost dropped his laundry basket. He quickly gathered himself and went over to her.

When Bob got within speaking distance, he asked, "Is anyone sitting in the seat beside you?"

Tina looked up from her phone. When she saw who was talking to her, she couldn't contain her smile.

Tina answered, "No. The seat is all yours."

After introducing himself and talking about their different majors, Bob asked Tina what she liked to do when she wasn't in class or studying. When she mentioned that she enjoyed doing anything outside, Bob invited her to meet him at the College Amusement Center the next day to play putt-putt golf.

Bob was waiting for Tina when she arrived at the amusement center. He had already paid for the game because he wanted to make it clear to Tina that he was interested in her and was willing to put in the effort to make this a special occasion. Tina thanked him and was excited about the way things were starting off.

From their first date onward, Bob couldn't stop thinking about how Tina looked the last time he saw her, and Tina enjoyed remembering how she felt safe when Bob would wrap his arm around her shoulder as they walked through a crowd.

After dating for a few weeks, Bob and Tina both felt ready for the next step in their relationship. Bob brought wine and flowers over to Tina's place, and Tina bought a new lacy bra.

Shortly after their first night together, they switched off staying at each other's place during the weekend. On Friday nights, they would sleep at Bob's place; on Saturday nights, Bob would sleep over at Tina's place.

Bob was an early riser, waking up at 6 a.m. every day, even on weekends. He started his day with a run. By 7 o'clock, he'd be back home and in the shower, blasting music.

Saturday mornings, to Tina, were not just a cessation of alarms and deadlines but a time to burrow herself in blankets and pillows. She would lie in bed until 10 a.m., sometimes even later, and enjoy not feeling like she had to rush. But now that Tina was dating Bob, she didn't mind being woken up early; she cherished every moment she spent with him.

On Saturday nights, Bob enjoyed the look on Tina's face as he took the first bite of the delicious meal she prepared for him. Her eyes would dance with mischief as she became a culinary sorceress, each dish a spell cast with flavor and laughter.

Whenever Tina cooked, chaos would reign in the kitchen. Pots and pans would fill the sink, their greasy contents threatening to spill onto the counter. Flour would dust the countertops, and splattered sauces would paint the walls.

Bob wasn't the kind of guy who'd protest about a stray sock on the floor, but the faint echo of his mother's voice, "Everything in its place!" still nagged at the back of his mind whenever dishes sat unwashed in the sink.

Bob and Tina were aware of each other's quirks, but they couldn't imagine anything worth arguing about. Being on different sleep schedules and piles of dirty dishes in the sink weren't important. Everything felt right between them, and they didn't want anything to spoil it.

As graduation approached, Bob and Tina started discussing their plans for the future. Initially, they considered moving in together to save money, as they enjoyed spending time together. But after discussing it, they realized they couldn't imagine life without each other, so they started planning a wedding.

The first year of their marriage was suffused with the same lust and passion as their honeymoon. Some weekends, they would shower only to slip back into their panties and underwear, respectively. They had each other's complete attention.

Reality began to set in during the second year of marriage when Tina and Bob realized they had different approaches to money. Tina loved the feeling of finding a new and unique item that she just had to have. Whether it was a piece of clothing, a home decor item, or even a new gadget, Tina was always on the lookout for something new. Bob, on the other hand, was more focused on saving money for a rainy day.

One morning, Bob's routine of stretching before his run took a nose-dive when his eyes landed on the laptop. Tina had left it open on the kitchen counter; the screen displayed thousands of dollars' worth of charges on their credit card.

Bob wanted to avoid arguing with Tina about money, so he postponed the conversation until the weekend, when he believed that they would have more time to calmly discuss the matter. On Saturday morning, Bob finished his cereal and waited until Tina had almost finished her grapefruit before starting the conversation.

He cleared his throat and said, "I believe that when we work together as a team, we can accomplish anything."

Tina looked at Bob. *I wonder where this is coming from,* she thought.

"I feel the same way, but you sound so serious."

"It is serious to me," Bob said. "I never want to feel like I did when I was a child."

This entire conversation was so unexpected. Tina tried to imagine what Bob was going on about, but she couldn't come up with an answer.

"You have to tell me what you're talking about. I don't understand."

"I want to talk about money—saving money and spending money."

"You don't need to worry about that," Tina interjected. "We are both earning a good salary. We will never be homeless or go hungry."

The suggestion that money would never be a problem didn't put Bob at ease. Instead, it made him concerned about how fast things could get out of control.

"You might be right about us having good jobs, but debt can feel like a weight hanging over your head, and it can be hard to see a way out."

"Debt is a part of life," Tina replied. "Everybody I know has credit card debt or, at the very least, a car payment."

Bob interjected, "I'm not saying we can't make ends meet or we're leaving bills unpaid."

"What exactly are you saying?"

After a thoughtful moment, Bob drew a long breath and stood up from the kitchen table. He was too agitated to sit in a chair. He walked over to the counter and leaned back on it.

"When I was in the ninth grade, my dad got laid off when his company was downsizing. I remember wanting to play football that year, but my parents didn't have the three hundred dollars to cover the cost of dry cleaning the uniforms and transportation to the away games. I could have asked the coach if there was another way to pay, but I was too embarrassed. I remember telling myself that I never wanted to feel that way again."

"You never told me that before," Tina said.

Feeling more relaxed after explaining where some of his anxiety about money came from, Bob sat back down at the table.

Bob continued, "We didn't lose our house, but I remember my father tearing up bills and throwing them in the trash. He would tell my mom that the company would resend the bill the next month. Watching everything that happened made me want to be careful with money."

Money never crossed Tina's mind as a problem or an advantage growing up. She couldn't recall ever having heard her parents discuss money.

"I remember growing up, my mom had a stack of credit cards in her purse with a rubber band around them. They almost looked like a deck of playing cards."

"That would be terrifying to me," Bob exclaimed.

"Oh, and my dad brought me a new toy every Friday when I was a kid," Tina said. "I was always excited to see what he would bring me."

Bob scooted his chair closer to Tina. He took her hands and held them inside of his.

"It sounds like we both have a very complicated relationship with money. You're a spender, and I'm a saver."

"That's true. We're different."

Feeling grateful that money hadn't caused an argument, Bob smiled and winked at Tina.

"I've figured out a way to tackle this together. We can each have two accounts, one individual and one joint. This way, we can use our personal accounts for our individual expenses while the joint account can be used for savings and paying bills. You can go shopping with your personal account, and I can have peace of mind knowing that we are saving money for unexpected situations."

Two years later, Tina and Bob had saved enough money for a down payment, so they bought a house and started a family. While on maternity leave, Tina felt like she should take on most of the responsibilities for the home and the children. After all, she was home all day, and it made sense for her to take care of things. But after returning to work, Tina continued to shoulder most of the caregiving and household duties.

When Tina returned to work after her second maternity leave, her company offered her a job promotion, but she turned it down. Between working forty hours a week, getting the kids ready in the morning, and making sure she spent some quality time with them after she picked them up from daycare, Tina was exhausted and didn't have room for anything else in her schedule.

Bob, on the other hand, was ambitious and eager to advance his career. He took on extra projects, which caused him to put in even longer hours at work. Bob was leaving the house before Tina woke up and came home late. He was determined to get promoted, but he missed spending time with his wife.

The differences between Bob's and Tina's schedules and demands carried over into the bedroom. Bob's sexual appetite hadn't changed, but Tina found it hard to make that leap from the five minutes after she got the kids asleep to Bob's wanting to have sex. She resented Bob for thinking it was easy for her to set aside time to have sex.

Tina thought, *What happened to the romantic Bob who used to bring me flowers?*

Bob truly appreciated Tina's support during his long work hours. To show his gratitude, he arranged to have dinner delivered to their home three nights a week. Despite his efforts, he often found himself cleaning the kitchen before they could enjoy their meal on the nights he took care of dinner. Bob had mentioned to Tina several times that he saw the kitchen as a shared space that needed to be kept clean, but Tina's habit of leaving dirty pots and pans on the stove and dishes in the sink continued.

Considering Tina's blatant disregard for his expectations about keeping a kitchen clean and her cold reaction to his sexual advances time and time again, Bob started to wonder if he and Tina had ever been compatible. Bob couldn't decide if Tina was falling out of love with him or if he was falling out of love with her.

Tina was also starting to have questions about the relationship. She resented Bob for waiting for her to ask him to do things with the children or around the house instead of taking the initiative. Some days, she felt like she was always the one doing everything.

A few months after Tina and Bob got married, they took a trip to Atlantic City. One night, they went to the bar for a drink, where they met an older couple who had been married for thirty-four years. They asked them what the secret was to a long marriage. The older couple agreed that the secret was simply not to get a divorce.

Bob and Tina were both individually reflecting on that weekend in Atlantic City. They felt like divorce might be the best answer for them as a couple, but they couldn't decide if a divorce was the best thing for the children. Without discussing it, they both decided to take the older couple's advice from Atlantic City and stay together.

But over time, Bob and Tina couldn't shake the feeling of being stuck. Their unhappy marriage was creating a difficult situation, and it wasn't easy for either of them to know what to do.

Bob struggled to cope with Tina's rejection of his sexual advances. His ego went into self-protect mode and told him to look for someone else who would want him. There were women at work, and the barista at the coffee bar was hot. The problem was that he wasn't a cheater. He would have to be divorced before he could be with another woman.

Tina tried shopping to cope with her frustration, but she quickly lost interest in what she bought for herself after she got it home. Three shirts were hanging in her closet with the tags still on them because nothing she bought made her relationship with Bob any better.

The following Saturday afternoon, everything came to a head. Tina was at home with the children. She spent the day changing the linen on all the beds and doing laundry. Bob took the grocery list and went to the store. On his way home, he picked up the dry cleaning and stopped at the pet store for some dog food.

By the time Bob got home, the cargo section in the SUV was full. He started carrying the groceries into the kitchen when he noticed the kitchen sink was overflowing with dirty dishes. Tina had stacked more dirty dishes and plates on the counter beside the sink.

Bob continued carrying in the groceries, thinking about how, just last Saturday, he had spoken to Tina about how the messy kitchen made it difficult to put away the groceries. With each bag of groceries Bob carried into the house, he grew madder and madder.

When Tina walked into the kitchen, Bob snapped, "I did all the shopping, so the least you can do is put the groceries away in this messy kitchen."

Later that afternoon, when the kids lay down for their nap, Tina went to find Bob. Even though it had been over an hour since she put the groceries away, she was still mad at Bob for being short with her when he got home from shopping.

"You seem to think I'm some kind of multi-tasking machine," Tina exclaimed. "You expect me to take care of the kids and clean up the house while at the same time making sure that all the dishes are clean just so you stay happy."

Feeling disrespected, Bob blurted out, "What are you talking about? The kitchen is always a mess."

Tina was becoming impatient. She looked at the clock. She still had clothes to fold, and the kids would want to eat dinner after they woke up from their nap. .

"I'm not your maid," Tina proclaimed. "If you see something dirty, why don't you clean it up? I shouldn't have to point everything out to you."

"Wait a minute, Tina! I've told you lots of times that I don't particularly appreciate putting away groceries or sitting down to eat in a messy kitchen. I'll admit that I noticed that you didn't clean up your kitchen before we got married, but now I don't feel like you are working with me on this."

Suddenly, Tina had a revelation. She was mad at Bob for not acknowledging everything she did, but she was doing the same thing by not accepting how important his concerns were to him.

Immediately regretting leaving the kitchen in a mess, Tina said, "You're right. I should have straightened up the kitchen before you got home with the groceries."

Hearing affection in his wife's voice, Bob quickly responded, "I don't want to be right. I want you to see me like you did when we were dating."

"I want that too," Tina said. "I need to feel like you care about me."

"You know I care."

"I believe you do, but you don't show it," Tina said.

"What do you mean? I'm trying to get a promotion so we have more money. That way, we can take more vacations and get away together."

"That's not what I'm talking about, Bob. You used to come up behind me while I was cooking and grab me. Then, you would flip me around and kiss me. I felt loved then. Now you want me to jump into the bed with you after I've spent an hour getting the kids ready for bed and cleaning up their messes."

Bob wondered how he had gotten Tina's lack of passion so wrong. "I didn't know that you felt this way. I stopped trying to initiate anything because I thought you had lost interest."

"Never! I'm just tired."

Bob, feeling compelled to acknowledge his shortcomings, said, "I've been consumed with getting ahead and lost my focus on us. I'm sorry I made you feel like I was ignoring you."

Longing for those old feelings, Tina said, "I need to tell you more that I appreciate everything you do for us."

"I love you. You are the sexiest woman that I have ever known."

Tina walked over and whispered in Bob's ear. "The children should be asleep for at least another hour."

Bob and Tina weren't blindly pressing forward, thinking that paying bills and cleaning up the dishes after dinner would be exciting. But, at the same time, neither one wanted to be like the couple they met in Atlantic City. They didn't want to stay married by simply not getting a divorce. They wanted to be faithful and tender with each other in the good and bad times, just like they promised when they married.

On their fiftieth wedding anniversary, Bob and Tina looked back on their lives with great pride and joy. Bob still called Tina the sexiest woman alive, and Tina snuggled up close to Bob every chance she got. Not only had they made it as a family, but they had also made it as a couple.

SECOND PLACE EMOTIONS

Emma's lips quivered as she curled up in the floorboard behind the passenger seat. She was trying to hold back her tears but couldn't help but sniffle.

Just before Emma got into the car, her grandmother had asked her, "Do you think your parents treat you and your brother differently?"

At that moment, the only thing that Emma could think of was how she was expected to do as she was told while her brother was allowed some say in how things went.

Emma answered, "Sometimes, I do."

"Do you know why they treat you differently?"

Emma wasn't exactly sure why they treated them differently. But she knew that if she spoke up like her brother did, she would be punished and told she was a bad girl.

Unable to explain her parents' reasoning, Emma answered, "No. I don't know why."

By this time, Emma's grandmother knew that if Emma started asking questions, she wouldn't have the time to answer them.

She smiled at Emma and said, "I think you are very smart. We'll talk more about this the next time I see you."

Emma stayed hidden down by the floorboard until she felt like she wouldn't cry anymore. After wiping her runny nose on her shirt, she climbed onto the seat.

As the car pulled out of her grandmother's driveway, Emma's brother watched his hand being pushed up and down by the wind as he held it out the window. Emma's parents were in the front seat. They had heard Emma whimpering earlier but had ignored it. They knew she was upset about leaving her grandmother, but they also knew she would stop crying soon enough.

On the car ride home, Emma's brother's voice crackled with excitement as he rattled off tales of late-night bonfires, the putt-putt golf championship he won, and skiing at the lake. Emma was curious about how the summers back home had continued without her, but at the same time, she couldn't help thinking about the good times she had building forts with her grandfather and telling her grandmother stories about the things she had found in the woods. Emma wished she could stay with her grandparents forever and never have to say goodbye.

A few weeks before her parents came to take her back home, Emma and her cousin started asking her uncle when the watermelons would be ripe. After listening to their constant pestering for two days, Emma's uncle told them he knew a secret way to tell if a watermelon was ripe.

The first step was to find the most enormous watermelon in the field. Then, you roll it over and cut a plug about an inch deep into it. When you pull it out, the watermelon is ripe if the plug is red. The watermelon needs to stay in the field longer if the plug has any green. The secret trick was to stick the plug back into the watermelon if it wasn't ripe, then roll it back over so it could continue to grow.

Eager to test their uncle's trick, Emma and her cousin took a sharp knife from the kitchen and went to the field where her grandfather had planted the watermelons. They cut a plug in the biggest watermelon they could find. The watermelon was green, so they stuck the pug back into the hole. They ended up cutting plugs in every watermelon in the garden.

Two days later, Emma's grandfather was sitting on the porch, enjoying his morning coffee, when he smelled a sour smell coming from the watermelon patch. When he rolled the watermelons over to see where the smell was coming from, he discovered the plugs in all his watermelons.

Later that morning, when Emma went outside to play, she saw her grandfather in the watermelon patch. He was throwing watermelons into a hole that he had dug.

When Emma's grandfather saw her watching him, he called her over and said, "I know you cut the holes in the watermelons, but I'm not mad at you. I'm mad at your uncle for making up a story when he was drunk."

Emma felt terrible about ruining all the watermelons, but she was grateful that her grandfather didn't force her to take all the blame. Emma knew things would be different if her parents discovered what she had done. They would tell her that the ruined watermelons were her fault because she was a bad girl, and she would have believed her parents and felt ashamed.

Before Emma left the watermelon patch, her grandfather hugged her and told her not to listen to her uncle anymore.

When Emma returned home from her grandparents' house at the end of the summer, she had a ritual that she looked forward to—shopping for new school clothes with her mom. However, her excitement always turned to disappointment when her mom made the final decision on which outfits to buy.

The week before school started, Emma's cousin, Amelia, came to Emma's house to see her new school clothes. As Emma took her clothes out of the shopping bags, she learned that the father she had always known was her stepfather. Amelia told her that she was adopted.

Emma immediately lost interest in her new clothes and ran to find her mother. Emma's mother told her it was true, and she planned to tell her one day. Her father adopted her after her parents got married. That way, she would have the same last name as her brother.

While listening to her mother explain that she was indeed adopted, Emma wondered how Amelia knew her father was her stepfather before she did. She felt betrayed by her parents for not telling her before her cousin did. Emma quickly realized her grandmother was the only person she could trust to help her sort through all these new revelations.

Later that afternoon, Emma called her grandmother and told her she knew her brother was only her half-brother. Emma's grandmother reminded Emma that she had already tried to help her see the differences between herself and her brother and reassured her that both she and her grandfather loved her equally. She further explained to Emma that her parents had their own reasons for treating each child differently, and it wasn't because of anything either of them had done. Instead, they respond to them differently for reasons only they know.

Emma's grandmother succeeded at easing some of Emma's concerns, but Emma still had a lot of questions that she wanted to ask her mom about her birth father. But when her mother refused to discuss the topic any further, Emma decided not to bring it up again. She thought it would be best not to think about being adopted anymore but instead to focus on her friends and school work.

When Emma entered high school, she began preparing for the yearly ritual of shopping for new school clothes by rehearsing arguments in her head and practicing how to stand up for herself when her mom wanted to pick out her clothes. However, Emma knew her mother would make her feel guilty if she disagreed with any of her choices. So, instead of talking to her mom about her fashion sense, Emma asked if she could get a part-time job.

Emma was excited to start working at the local ice cream shop. She loved the sweet smells and the happy customers. With her first paycheck, she decided to update her school wardrobe. Emma needed new jeans, cute tops, and a new pair of sneakers.

Emma also wanted to find some fun outfits. Emma noticed a cute flower bikini in the window of a local shop. She bought the bikini and soon attracted the attention of a local boy named Matt.

After Emma and Matt started dating, Emma's mom made a point of letting Emma know that she would not be her babysitter if she got pregnant. Emma couldn't decide if her mom's comment was a threat to deter her from getting pregnant at a young age or a glimpse into her mom's resentment about being a single mom and missing out on things when Emma was first born. Either way, Emma just wanted to have fun with her new boyfriend.

On Friday nights, Matt and Emma would park Matt's car in one of the parking spaces at the local fast-food restaurant and people-watch. One night, while they watched their friends cruise around the parking lot, Matt asked Emma what caused her family to clutter up their house's front window with so many knick-knacks.

Emma had noticed that her mother started placing plastic flowers and cheap-looking figurines on the windowsill shortly after she began dating Matt. Emma didn't like the way it looked and found it tacky. When Matt expressed his dislike for it, Emma began to wonder if her mother was intentionally trying to make the house look unattractive in order to make Matt lose interest in her.

Feeling more confident about her opinion, Emma asked her mother, "Do you think all the different things in the front window ruin the house's appearance from the street?"

Emma's mother quickly dismissed her, saying, "Think about how much work I put into decorating the window sills. They are fine just the way they are."

Emma stopped saying anything about the knick-knacks, but the knick-knacks in the window became a silent war. Emma would take the knick-knacks out of the window and put them on the coffee table in the living room. Then, her mom would pick them up and put them back in the window. Emma found the moving back and forth with the knick-knacks to be annoying.

The last straw wasn't the tacky knick-knacks or Matt's thoughts about the knick-knacks. Instead, what infuriated Emma was the importance her mother assigned to the knick-knacks. Sure, it was her mother's house, but just once, couldn't what she wanted be important too?

The summer before Emma left for college, she and her family decided to go on a camping adventure at the beach. As the family drove down the winding road to the state park, Emma's parents reminisced about a summer camping trip they took with Emma's brother. Emma and her brother were in the back seat, each lost in their own world. Emma had her nose buried in a book while her brother watched the wind playfully push his hand up and down outside the car window.

The sun blazed down as Emma and her family arrived at the campsite. They sprang into action, pulling out the awning and extending the stabilizer jacks like a well-oiled machine. With the camper set up, Emma's mother packed some drinks into a cooler, and they all piled into the car to drive to the beach. Once they reached the shore, they spent hours surfing and building sandcastles, the waves crashing against the shore in a never-ending rhythm.

As the day wore on, hunger gnawed at their stomachs, and they decided to grab some food. As Emma and her family walked towards a restaurant tucked away between their beach chairs and a group of towering palm trees, they could smell the aroma of garlic and freshly baked bread escaping the open windows. After being seated at their table and looking over the menu, Emma and her family exchanged amused glances, eager to try a new dish.

After the last bite was devoured, Emma and her family decided to head to the bait shop to rent some fishing rods and grab some bait. But as they made their way to the pier, Emma had a different plan in mind. She had started reading a book on the drive to the park and was eager to finish it. So, she asked if they could drop her off at the camper to read while her family went fishing.

Around 9:30 that night, Emma's mother came back to the camper to check on her. She asked Emma if she wanted to fish at the pier, but Emma was enjoying reading her book.

Just before Emma's mother left for the pier, she turned the handle to lock the camper's door. Then, as she closed the door behind herself, Emma's mother told Emma to keep the camper's door locked.

After her mom left, Emma started thinking about how her mother had told her what clothes to pack for their camping trip, what would happen if she got pregnant, and now she was telling her to lock the camper door, but never considered her feelings, like the knick-knacks on the window sill.

Emma set her book down, then unlocked the door to the camper out of spite. She resented being treated like a child and was determined to show her mother that she was her own person and could make her own decisions.

Emma picked up her book and started reading but a few minutes later, there was something about the dark and the sounds in the woods that made Emma get up and lock the door again. Just as she was getting lost in the story, there was a knock at the door. Emma looked over at the door and saw the doorknob turning.

Emma asked, "Who is it?"

A man answered, "I'm looking for a light for a cigarette."

Emma said, "I don't have a light."

The man asked, "Do you want to come outside?"

Emma answered, "No."

Emma got scared when she heard the man leaning on the camper and saw him trying to look into several of the windows. She turned off the lights and lay down on the floor.

Eventually, the people in the campsite next door waved her to their site. They took her to the pier where her parents were. The park ranger came and looked around the campsite, but the man looking for a cigarette lighter was nowhere to be found.

The next day, when Emma went to the campground bathrooms to brush her teeth and wash her face, she was anxious that the stranger she had encountered the previous night might be lurking in one of the stalls. She wished she could share her fears with her parents, but she knew that her parents never really cared about her feelings, so she kept her worries to herself.

In the fall, Emma started college, and tailgating quickly became her favorite part of the college experience. Plate-loads of food and ice-cold beer always managed to show up. The wildly entertaining part was how the parking lot posse created new drinking games every time they waited to enter the stadium and take their seats.

When the final tailgating party of the season rolled around, Emma's friend approached her and told her that she wanted her to come to the party, but the stadium only allowed ten people per tailgating area. When Emma said she understood, her friend laughed at her and told her she was joking.

Emma had always considered her willingness to put the needs of others in front of her own to be one of her best assets. As a child, Emma would ignore her feelings and do what she thought her mother wanted her to do. Emma had done the same thing with her friend. She was hurt when her friend told her she couldn't attend the tailgating party, but she didn't get upset. She kept her feelings to herself.

The inconsistency between what her parents and her peers expected was very confusing. Emma's peers wanted something different than compliance from her, but Emma didn't understand what that something different was. She was angry at herself for how she felt and for not knowing how to act.

The anger that Emma felt towards herself morphed into anxiety. She couldn't stop thinking about how difficult expressing emotions was for her, but her friends tossed laughter and tears around like confetti. Emma sensed that it was only a matter of time before she would be labeled a social outcast.

Rather than waiting for the tailgaters to push her out somehow, Emma decided to look for new friends. She saw a flyer for exercise classes at the college gym and soon discovered she was meeting new people while doing something she enjoyed.

One afternoon, while Emma was at the gym, she found it difficult to remove the plates from the squat rack. Alan, another gym member, noticed her struggling and offered to help her. After doing a few sets together, they high-fived, feeling the rush of endorphins.

Alan leaned in, his voice low, "You're pretty impressive," he said.

Emma smirked, her eyes sparkling. "Not too shabby yourself," she countered.

Their playful banter continued as they stretched, their bodies close but not touching.

Finally, Alan took a chance. "So," he said, his voice a husky whisper, "how about we celebrate our awesomeness with some coffee? My treat."

Emma raised an eyebrow, a playful challenge in her gaze. "Hmm, I don't know," she teased. "You'll have to convince me."

Alan grinned, the challenge accepted. As they walked out of the gym, their laughter echoed in the air, making it clear that the real workout was just beginning.

Their coffee dates became a playground of playful banter and stolen glances. Alan would tease Emma about her latte art, and she'd counter with witty remarks about his caffeine addiction. One sunny morning, Alan challenged Emma to a latte art competition, the prize a stolen kiss. She aced it, of course, and as their lips met, the cafe faded away, replaced by a world of fizzing excitement.

Two years later, Alan took Emma to the same cozy cafe where they first had coffee. The aroma of freshly ground beans filled the air as Alan led Emma into the hidden garden behind the cafe. He stopped before a trellised archway and pulled out a small velvet box hidden in his pocket. The box clicked open, revealing a ring nestled on a bed of velvet. It was simple yet elegant, a single diamond catching the light.

Tears welled in Emma's eyes, a smile lighting up her face like a sunrise. "Yes," she whispered, her voice barely audible over Alan's pounding heart. "A thousand times, yes."

The world around them faded, replaced by the kaleidoscope of emotions swirling in their eyes. They stood there for a while, simply basking in the glow of their new reality.

Then, a playful glint entered Alan's eyes. "So," he said, his voice husky with emotion, "Celebratory coffee?"

As Emma sipped her hot coffee, one question weighed heavily on her mind: Who would walk her down the aisle on her wedding day? Emma's stepfather had been in her life since she was two. He had raised her as his own daughter, and she was grateful for everything he did. But still, Emma had always felt like something was missing.

Emma had never met her biological father and knew nothing about him, so she contemplated asking her mother about how to contact him so he could walk her down the aisle. But Emma was afraid that if she spoke to her mother about her feelings, her mother might ruin her wedding day by trying to make her feel guilty for going against her wishes.

After getting married, Emma strived to be the perfect wife, just like she had aspired to be the good girl, the daughter who would bend and shrink for those she loved. Emma wanted to please her husband, so she would agree with him to prevent an argument. He saw her agreeing as parroting. When she shared her opinion, fights usually broke out around Emma just not getting it. It was a double-edged sword. Go along and be accused of being a parrot. State your opinion and be accused of not getting it. Her best wasn't good enough.

Emma tried to talk to her mother about the arguments in her marriage, but her words fell on deaf ears. Her mother dismissed her feelings, attributing the problems in Emma's marriage to the inevitable stresses of life.

"All marriages have problems," her mother would say, her tone laced with exasperation. "Just get over it."

Emma and Alan had been married for ten years and had two children when Alan started to feel restless. He started applying for jobs in a different state and decided the family should move if he got a job offer.

After Alan told Emma about his plans, Emma thought about just waiting and hoping that things would miraculously work out, but at the same time, she worried about leaving her friends and family behind and finding a new job. Anytime Emma tried to express her concerns, her husband would get angry and accuse her of not supporting his dreams. Alan started feeling stuck in a relationship he no longer wanted, so he filed for divorce.

Since childhood, Emma had based her choices on how they would affect others. Her focus wasn't "What do I want or need" but rather, "What can I do to make you happy with me." Other people had always come first in Emma's life, so she wasn't sure if she could trust herself to know how she felt about her husband asking her for a divorce.

In the end, the divorce had the effect of reaffirming to Emma that she was inherently flawed. As a child, her parents couldn't wait to get rid of her for the summer. As an adult, she failed as a wife. And now, her children might become someone's stepchildren.

The reality of how awful things had become made Emma's days seem intolerable. Feeling overwhelmed, Emma started looking for a way to take her mind off things. Her favorite time of the day was five o'clock when she had a date with her new best friend, a bottle of wine.

Emma's escape from the shame of not feeling worthy of love began with a single bottle of wine. After a few glasses, fleeting dreams of being good enough would consume Emma.

Over time, one bottle of wine stopped chasing away the self-doubt, so Emma started drinking two bottles a night. The belief that other people could see her as a good person returned, but she woke up every morning feeling groggy and hung over. Emma managed to drag herself out of bed and get to work on time, but she was struggling. She would sit at her desk, feeling distracted by her pounding head and churning stomach. By noon, she wanted to go home and crawl into bed, but Emma knew she couldn't just leave work in the middle of the day.

Emma continued romanticizing the pain she had been holding onto for two more years. But, as the days grew longer and longer waiting on her five o'clock date, Emma came to realize her alcohol-induced delusions at night didn't keep her days from being filled with self-consciousness and despair.

Emma was smart enough to know that if she was going to stop drinking, she had to replace her old friend with something new. Walking around the neighborhood became the new five o'clock distraction.

One street in the neighborhood had a steep hill that curved around an empty lot. As Emma turned the corner, she saw a lady sitting in a rocking chair on the porch of her house, watching a small dog play in the yard.

Emma asked the lady, "What's your dog's name?"

The lady answered, "Tiny, and I'm Sylvia."

After Emma introduced herself, Sylvia invited her to sit on the porch and drink coffee with her. Emma accepted Sylvia's offer, so Sylvia went into the house and brought a pot of coffee and some sugar and cream on a tray outside. She set the tray on the table next to Emma and poured two cups of coffee. After asking Emma if she wanted cream or sugar, Sylvia sat down in the chair beside Emma.

"Tiny saved my life," Sylvia said with tears in her eyes. "I lost my husband eight months ago. We were married for thirty-four years. I miss him, and sometimes I feel lost. Tiny gives me a sense of purpose to fill my day."

Seeing the agony on Sylvia's face, Emma leaned over and gently put her hand on Sylvia's arm.

"I cannot imagine how you felt after losing your husband."

An expression of profound sadness moved across Sylvia's face. Then, with a fresh burst of tears, she said, "I believe that you could imagine just by the fact that you know some things have to be experienced to be understood."

Emma and Sylvia formed a friendship that replaced Emma's need to walk as a distraction to avoid alcohol. They started meeting at each other's houses a few times a week, and no matter where they met, the conversations were always lively.

Sylvia found that talking about her family helped her to cope with her grief over losing her husband. She told Emma how her husband had a five-year-old daughter when she married him. The child's mother left him for another man, so Sylvia's husband was left to raise his daughter alone.

Not wanting to be the cliché of a terrible stepmother, Sylvia tried to love her stepdaughter when she was young, like her own child. But the fact that she and her stepdaughter didn't share all the same experiences was enough to convince Sylvia that they would never be able to bond fully.

Despite all the angst when the children were growing up, Sylvia was now the closest to her stepdaughter. The two children Sylvia had with her husband resented how controlling she and their father had been during their childhood.

Emma always appreciated how open and honest Sylvia was about the things that happened in her life. Sylvia made it easy for Emma to trust her even though trust had always come as a challenge to Emma. Emma decided to try something new and be honest about her life.

"Growing up, I was always afraid of getting into trouble for 'arguing' with my parents. But I never felt like I was arguing; I just had a different opinion than my parents."

Sylvia realized how alike she and her husband were to Emma's parents, always insisting that the children do it their way, so Sylvia asked Emma for some insight.

Fidgeting with her hands, Sylvia hesitantly asked, "Did your parents' expectations for you to be a certain way make you question if you would ever be able to measure up?"

Emma knew that when someone asks you a question, they are often trying to understand themselves better. She wanted to help Sylvia on her journey, but at the same time, she didn't feel comfortable making a comment that could be interpreted as her judging Sylvia or her relationship with her children.

Emma answered, "It's complicated."

Appreciative of her friend's kindness, Sylvia smiled. But Sylvia still had one more question that she wanted to ask Emma.

"Do you think your experiences with your parents when you were younger affected any of your adult relationships?"

Reflecting on her previous relationships, Emma realized that it had always been about what the other person wanted. Feeling like she had been robbed of a clear sense of who she was, Emma got angry. The anger was painful but also enlivening, like a strong cup of coffee.

"The way I learned to behave as a child became a bad habit that carried over into many of my adult relationships. The thing with a bad habit is that it can be useful when it helps you to cope. It's like when you swear.

Swearing is a bad habit, but it does relieve frustration. My bad habit was ignoring what I thought and felt. But it just made me angry at myself and resentful of other people."

Listening to Emma talk reminded Sylvia of a time when she was in college, and her parents threatened to stop her allowance if she went with her friends to a weekend music festival. Sylvia had always wondered why her parents didn't trust her to make good decisions, but in hindsight, she realized that she and her husband had done the same thing with their children.

Sylvia shamefully admitted, "I don't understand how I could have been so controlling with my children when I knew how much I hated it when it was happening to me. The sad thing is that when you're growing up, you don't have any choice but to accept it."

Reflecting on her own life, Emma said, "It messes with your mind when love and acceptance are conditioned on being what the other person wants you to be."

"You're right," Sylvia said.

"I grew up feeling trapped," Emma said. "Sometimes, I would whisper to myself, *Get back in your cage to hide my* true thoughts and feelings from myself. But, do you want to know the worst part?"

"Sure."

"I became comfortable with being numb," Emma said. "That way, I didn't have to face the shame of not standing up for myself."

"It's important to remember that we were kids," Sylvia said.

Emma's thoughts turned to when she was a girl and would spend her summers at her grandparents' house.

Tears began to spill out of Emma's eyes when she said, "When I think of home, my heart goes to my grandparents. My grandfather didn't have much to say, but I always knew everything would be okay when he was there. My grandmother was my saving grace. She showed me that some-body could love me, that I was good enough to be loved."

"It's really something the way that one person can make such a big difference in a child's life," Sylvia said.

Appreciating Sylvia's support and admiring her courage to question her behaviors and beliefs, Emma felt compelled to say, "Knowing the person that you are, I don't believe you ever meant to hurt your children. It sounds like you were repeating the same parenting style that your parents used. Maybe my parents were doing the same thing, or maybe they saw me as different, but either way, I'm still hurt. I never felt like I was seen or understood at a deep level. I never felt safe putting myself first."

"It's sad that a person can cause a child to question their self-worth," Sylvia said

"Everyone has a past spent with their parents in childhood," Emma said. "But it's up to each individual to decide their future."

Later that afternoon, as Emma drove to the school to pick up her children, she thought about how she had been so focused on protecting her children from the pain of being an undervalued stepchild that she had completely ignored everything else. She had allowed the fighting in her marriage and her subsequent drinking to escape her negative feelings about herself to cause her children unneeded grief. It could have all been avoided if she had been true to herself instead of changing herself to make everyone else happy.

Emma pulled up in front of the school, joining the line of cars wait-ing for their children to be dismissed from school. A few minutes later, the door to the school opened, and Emma watched her children running towards the car. The children put their backpacks in the trunk and got into the car's back seat.

As Emma merged into traffic, she looked in the rearview mirror to check for any cars, but instead of seeing the road behind her, she saw her children looking at their phones. Looking at their precious faces, Emma felt compelled to dispel any rigid beliefs she might have unknowingly instilled in her children.

After driving for ten minutes, Emma and her children turned on the road, leading them into their neighborhood. As they drove down the tree-lined street, Emma reached over and turned the radio off. The silence made her children stop looking at their phones and look at her.

"I need to talk to you," Emma said.

Her children looked at each other, then back at her. "What is it?" her daughter asked.

"I've been thinking a lot lately about our family," Emma said. "We're always running around, doing things, and we never have any time to just sit down and talk to each other."

"It's so quiet in the car," her son said. "You might as well go ahead and tell us what you're thinking about now."

"I wanted to share something with you that I had to learn the hard way."

"Okay," her son said.

"Okay," her daughter said.

Emma took a deep breath and said, "I hope you always choose you. Of course, it's important to be considerate of other people, but if you start putting other people in front of your own happiness, you could start to feel guilty about wanting to be happy."

Emma's children sighed, ". . . oh, Mom!" But still, they heard every word she said. They felt relieved knowing they could go to their mom when they needed her. Even if it was something that might not be okay with her.

Conversations over coffee never ended between Emma and Sylvia. Yet, even with all the caffeine, the talks always seemed to settle them.

THE OTHER SIDE OF THE STREET

The whistle echoed through the gym, indicating the end of the PE class. As Zack looked around, he noticed three basketballs that had rolled beneath the bleachers. He picked them up one by one and placed them in the storage closet at the back of the gym. After scanning the gym again and finding no other stray balls, Zack wiped the sweat from his forehead and quickly headed to the water fountain for a drink.

All Zack wanted was a cool drink of water from the water fountain. But when he got there, two people were in line ahead of him. Everyone else in Zack's class had already gotten their drinks and stood against the gym wall, waiting for the teacher to let them into the locker room so they could shower and change.

Two of Zack's classmates, Wyatt and Bill, stood beside each other in line, waiting to enter the locker room. Earlier, Wyatt had smacked Bill's hand when Bill tried to steal the basketball from him.

Bill looked at Wyatt and said, "You better never touch me like that again."

Wyatt knew from past experiences that Bill was about to give him a wedgie, so he took off running. Bill chased after him, determined to teach Wyatt a lesson.

Wyatt's heart was pounding as he tried to move faster. He could hear Bill's footsteps echoing behind him, and he knew he couldn't maintain this pace for much longer. When Wyatt turned his head to see how close Bill was, he accidentally bumped into Zack and one of the other boys waiting in line at the water fountain. Although Wyatt just brushed past Zack, the other boy lost his balance and fell to the ground.

As Zack stretched out his hand to help the other boy get off the floor, he glanced over at his classmates standing up against the gym wall. They were looking at him to see what he was going to do.

Zack didn't want to risk being teased by his friends for being easy on gay guys, so he punched Wyatt in the face. Wyatt was caught off guard, and he fell to the ground. Zack started kicking Wyatt while he was down. Wyatt tried to cover his head, but Zack was relentless.

A teacher saw what was happening and ran over to break up the fight. Zack was pulled away from Wyatt, and the teacher helped Wyatt to his feet.

The teacher took Zack to the principal's office, and Wyatt went to the nurse's office to get his injuries cleaned up. The principal suspended Zack for a week, and Wyatt was given a day off from school to recover.

That night at dinner, feeling a little guilty about the bloody nose he'd given Wyatt and the look of fear in the boy's eyes, Zack said to his father, "It's unfair that I got suspended for a week. Wyatt doesn't even want to be like the other boys; he would rather act like a girl."

"You did the right thing," Zack's father said. "You can't let a weak pansy push you around. What would people think?"

The next day, Zack's father told Zack he was proud of him for standing up for what's right. As a reward for holding Wyatt responsible for bumping into him, he gave Zack a new video game for his game console, and then he told Zack a story.

When Zack's father was Zack's age, an older gay man moved back in with his mother, and talk started around town that this guy's gayness could rub off on children. Some of the guys in the neighborhood, including Zack's grandfather, threatened to beat him up if they saw him out and about, running errands or meeting friends. They made the gay man so scared that he and his mom moved and were never seen again in the town.

Zack felt a little uneasy listening to his father talk about his grandfather threatening someone, but gaining and keeping his father's approval was very important to him. So, whenever his father said anything positive or negative about any subject, Zack quickly agreed with him.

Although there was no doubt about his father's opinions on certain topics, Zack wasn't sure about his father's opinion on gay girls. His father had never spoken to him about it.

Lily was a girl in Zack's school, rumored to be a lesbian. None of the guys believed the rumors because Lily was too pretty to be a lesbian. Instead, talk in the boy's locker room often centered on who would be the lucky guy to take Lily out on a date.

The girls at school had a completely different response to the rumors about Lily. They accused her of saying that she liked girls to get attention from boys.

Lily ignored all the rumors until one day, after a very competitive volleyball game with another class, she returned to the locker room to find that her clothes were missing. A note in her locker said, *Lucky Lesbo Lily.* Lily skipped taking a shower that day because she had no fresh clothes to change into, and the ones she had on smelled like sweat.

Another time, she found a note in her locker that offered to pay her fifty dollars if the guys' soccer team could watch her make out with another girl. The boys didn't come into the girl's locker room, so Lily knew it had to have been a girl who put the note in her locker. Lily understood that girls could be cruel, but writing a message like that was despicable.

The lesbian rumors started when Lily was thirteen years old. She kissed another girl on the lips after their team won a soccer match. Lily told herself that she had reacted like that because she wanted to be like the other girl. The other girl was cool, and she wanted to be her friend.

When Lily was sixteen, she started having vivid dreams about making out with a girl. Lily told herself that she was going through some adolescent phase that everyone went through, but at the same time, she was concerned about appearing weird, so when James asked her out, she said yes.

Lily found James to be okay, but mostly she wanted to test how she felt about boys. Lily and James ended up having sex together. Lily enjoyed her experience with James but wasn't sure if she wanted to repeat it.

Following an unsuccessful experiment with James, Lily began sharing articles supporting LGBTQ rights online. Lily's social media made some boys speculate that she had a secret girlfriend at school, while some girls believed she was seeking attention from James after their breakup.

Zack had known Lily in elementary school long before the lesbian rumors started. Now that they were both in high school, they would occasionally eat lunch together or run into each other at a party.

The other guys at school would tease Zack that he was trying to transform Lily into a "real" girl who only liked him, but he just wanted Lily's friendship. Being the school's star basketball player, Zack had more than enough girls who wanted to be his girlfriend.

The tipping point came for Lily when a straight girl approached her. She wanted to experiment with girls and asked Lily to try having sex with her. The girl's disrespectful approach infuriated Lily and gave her the courage to come out.

After Lily posted online that she was gay, Zack felt differently towards her. He was drawn to Lily's honesty and willingness to be open, which made her all the more interesting to him. Whenever someone attempted to mock or ridicule her, Zack was always there to defend her. His protective nature wasn't only grounded in a gallant stand; he also respected her, even though they happened to see the world differently.

During his final year in high school, Zack was offered a basketball scholarship to attend a state college. Once he arrived on campus, he began attending various fraternity parties. Shortly after that, he received an invitation to join a fraternity, and before long, his weekends were full of parties with lots of girls and alcohol.

Connor, another fraternity member, and Zack quickly became friends. Being first-year students and away from home for the first time, they seemed to understand each other's reactions to their new experiences in college. If Connor struggled to make friends, Zack was always there to listen and offer advice. And if Zack was feeling overwhelmed by his new classes, Connor knew how to calm him down and get him back on track.

One night, Connor stopped by Zack's dorm room with a bottle of rum. One of their favorite football teams was playing in a championship game.

"I thought we could watch the game and have a few drinks," Connor said.

Zack smiled. "That sounds great," he said.

They opened the bottle of rum and poured themselves some drinks. Zack turned on the TV, and they sat down on the bed, ready to watch the game.

The game was close, and both teams were playing well. Zack and Connor were cheering and yelling at the TV.

"Did you see the linebacker tackle that guy?" Connor asked. "He's so muscular."

"Yeah, he's a beast," Zack said.

Connor continued, "I often wonder what it would be like to be with another guy?"

Zack stopped looking at the TV and looked at Connor.

Connor asked, "Have you ever been with a guy?"

Zack had noticed pangs of arousal when he saw other men around campus, so feeling at ease with Connor, he decided to be truthful and said, "I've never done it, but I've thought about it."

The next thing that Zack and Connor knew was that they were kissing, and they had pulled their pants down to their knees. After they finished mutually masturbating, Connor felt unsure of how Zack felt about what had happened, so he pulled up his pants and left.

Zack felt very unsettled after his sexual encounter with Connor. Zack had always told himself that he wasn't gay, so now he was ashamed of himself and felt guilty for abusing his newfound freedom at college.

The following Saturday night, Zack ran into Connor at a fraternity party. They couldn't stop looking around while they were talking to each other. They were each concerned that the other one might say something they wouldn't want someone walking by to hear. After a few minutes, the worry about what might happen subsided. They fell back into their old routine. They started talking about football teams and commenting on how all the hot girls at the party looked.

Zack spotted Connor engrossed in his laptop screen as he entered the library a few days later. Zack knew that if he and Connor wanted to keep their friendship intact, they would have to have a conversation about what had happened between them. However, Zack hesitated to approach Connor in the library because he didn't want anyone else to overhear their conversation. So he opted to text Connor and asked if they could meet up to discuss things. After exchanging several texts, they agreed to meet at the park, where they could talk freely without any distractions.

After engaging in some small talk to get past the initial awkwardness, Zack couldn't stop himself from confessing to Connor that he had been crushing on him since they had masturbated together. Connor excited him to the degree that a girl never had. Connor looked at Zack with a scared look that seemed to say, are you sure?

Zack and Connor continued to go to the weekend fraternity parties as a way to keep their gay identities a secret from their fraternity brothers. If a woman ever pressured them to hook up while they were at a party, they would quickly find an excuse to leave. They wanted to keep up appearances while keeping their relationship exclusive.

Each time Zack met with Connor, he would hear his father's voice in his head telling him that gay guys were weak. Zack didn't think of himself as gay or weak. He mostly thought about how his family and friends would treat him as an outcast if they knew he was going out with Connor.

Speculation about Zack and Connor's relationship was running rampant on campus. Everyone had a theory about what was happening between them, but no one knew for sure.

Some people thought they were just friends, while others thought they were secretly dating. There were even some people who thought they were cousins.

Joe, a fellow fraternity brother, wanted to know if the rumors about Zack and Connor being gay were true. One day, as he passed Connor in the stairway, he stepped in front of him, blocking his path. After placing his hand on Connors's shoulder, trapping him against the rough brick wall, he leaned in close to Connor and asked, "Is that gay swingers club coming in between you and Zack?"

Conner pushed Joe away and asked, "Why do you care so much about my relationship with Zack?"

Joe interpreted Connor's response as a way to warn him that Zack was his boyfriend and he better keep his hands off. Suddenly, Connor and Zack were being outed as a couple at the fraternity and around campus.

Zack denied being gay and insisted that Connor get on board and tell people that the rumors weren't true. Connor responded by giving Zack an ultimatum: admit he was gay, or the relationship was over. Zack wasn't ready to acknowledge his homosexuality, even to himself, so Connor ended the relationship.

After everything that happened, Zack knew he needed some help, but he didn't know where to turn. Zack debated calling his parents, but he knew that being open with his parents about his relationship with Connor would take more courage than he could imagine.

Zack thought, *Even if I gathered the strength to talk to my parents, my father would probably disown me, and my mom would tell me that I was going to hell.* And Zack worried that he might even agree with his mom on some level.

Given the circumstances, the only option that made sense to Zack was to prove to himself and others that he was straight. He became a convincing heterosexual male when he mimicked other guys' reactions to seeing a girl in a bikini or an adult magazine. But when Zack caught himself looking at another man with interest, he would become overwhelmed with fear. Zack could not accept that he was the kind of person his father hated.

For several months, Zack spent a lot of time in his dorm room, staring at the wall. He had been feeling lonely and disconnected for a while now, but lately, it was getting worse. Despite being a popular basketball player, surrounded by girls, and seemingly having the time of his life, he was struggling. When Zack realized that the world wasn't going to end because he was gay but that he kind of wished that it would, he knew that he had to get some help.

Zack reached out to his old high school friend, Lily. Lily was surprised by Zack's revelation that he was gay, but she was thankful he trusted her enough to come out to her. Lily encouraged Zack by telling him she had lots of gay and straight friends. Still, she also warned Zack some people only focus on sex when it comes to gay relationships and fail to understand that people in a homosexual relationship provide each other with support and love, just like in a heterosexual relationship.

Listening to Lily, Zack started to feel uneasy, knowing that his parents would never accept the idea of him having a male as a partner. The only person Zack could think of in his family he could talk to was his older brother, Trevor. Trevor had always made Zack feel like he was really listening, not just going through the motions.

A few weeks later, Zack caught Trevor shooting hoops in the driveway. He had been rehearsing what he would say to Trevor for days and knew he couldn't keep putting it off any longer.

Zack took a deep breath and walked over to Trevor. "Hey," he said. "Can I talk to you for a minute?"

Trevor stopped shooting hoops and turned to look at Zack. "Sure," he said. "What's up?"

Zack hesitated for a moment. "I... I have something to tell you," he said. "And I'm really nervous about it."

Trevor's expression became serious. "What is it?" he asked.

Zack took another deep breath. "I've been struggling with something for a while, and I've finally come to terms with it. I'm gay."

Trevor paused, then said, "I'm...I'm not sure what to say."

"I know this is hard for you to understand, but I'm still the same person I've always been," Zack said. "I just happen to be gay."

Trevor paused again and said, "I...I can understand that."

"I'm glad you can understand," Zack said. "I was really worried about how you would react."

Trevor put his arm around Zack's shoulder, looked him in the eyes, and said, "I'm still your brother, Zack. I love you no matter what."

"Thanks, Trevor," Zack said. "I needed to hear that."

Worried about his brother's safety, Trevor said, "I've heard stories about how some guys can be cruel to people when they come out."

"I know," Zack said. "It's not always easy, but I'm trying to be my true self."

"That's all anyone can ask," Trevor said. "And if anyone ever does say anything wrong to you, just let me know. I'm always here for you."

"Thanks, Trevor. I really mean it."

A few weeks later, Trevor heard through the grapevine that Daniel, one of Zack's high school friends, had been calling him derogatory names behind his back. Trevor phoned Daniel to tell him he wouldn't tolerate anyone disrespecting his brother. Unbeknownst to Trevor, he had been on speakerphone, and several of the guys from high school had overheard the conversation.

When Daniel asked Trevor if Zack was gay, Trevor answered, "That's a question you need to ask Zack. But I will tell you that Zack has my support, no matter what."

After Zack's basketball buddies overheard the conversation between Trevor and Daniel, several of them decided to add fuel to the fire about Zack being gay. They took some of Zack's pictures from high school and posted them online. After Zack found the images of himself online with a link to different gay porn sites, he understood why so many of his friends were making excuses about being too busy to hang out with him.

All the adverse reactions Zack got for being homosexual caused him to question whether he should have ever admitted to being gay. Zack thought, *I still might be able to find a way to hide my desire for men from myself.* But deep inside, Zack knew he couldn't change how he felt. Zack became convinced that no matter what he did, it was only a matter of time until his own parents hated him.

The next thing Zack knew, he was waking up in an unfamiliar room. The bed that he was lying in seemed to dominate the space. The only other furniture was a bedside table, a comfortable chair, and what looked like a dining room chair. Zack started to get out of bed and find out where he was, but then as he pushed the covers off, he noticed a plastic band on his wrist. Suddenly, the smell of disinfectant and the sight of his gown brought everything into focus.

As Zack tried to recall why he was in the hospital, the door to his room abruptly opened. A nurse walked into his room and reminded him of the importance of getting some rest. When Zack asked the nurse what had happened, she only reassured him that the doctor would be in soon.

Thirty minutes later, the doctor came into Zack's room and told him that a guy in his college dorm had called 911 after finding him overdosed on tranquilizers. The doctors in the ER had to pump his stomach to save his life. After all that happened, Zack would have to stay in the hospital for at least the next three days. The doctor assured Zack that he was safe and would get the help he needed.

At the same time the doctor was walking out of Zack's room, Lily was stepping through the double glass doors leading into the hospital. Lily asked the volunteer at the information desk for directions to the ward where Zack was. The receptionist gave her a map and told her the ward was on the third floor.

Lily took the map and headed towards the elevator. She pressed the button for the third floor, and the elevator started to go up. When the elevator reached the third floor, Lily got out and looked around. She saw a sign that said "Psychiatric Ward," and she followed the sign to the nurse's station.

Once Lily got to Zack's ward, she showed the receptionist her driver's license and told her she was there to see Zack. The receptionist checked her computer and then gave Lily a locker key. Lily was told to lock her purse and cell phone in the locker on the wall behind the receptionist's desk and then return the key.

Lily found the locker on the wall that matched the number on her key. She opened the locker and put her things inside. After she locked her things up, she returned the key to the receptionist.

The receptionist explained, "I'll hold the locker's key until after the visit. We don't want the patients to get access to anything they might use to hurt themselves or someone else."

"I see."

The receptionist continued, "You can have a seat in the waiting room. A nurse will have to escort you to Zack's room."

Eventually, a nurse came to take Lily to where Zack was. Lily followed the nurse down the hall through several locked doors. At each door, the nurse would stop and punch the numbers into a keypad as they went farther back into the building.

Zack was tossing and turning, trying to fall asleep, when the door to his room opened. Zack opened his eyes and saw Lily standing in the doorway. She smiled at him, and he smiled back. Lily made her way over to the chair next to Zack's bed and sat down.

"Hey," Lily said. "How are you feeling?"

"I'm okay," Zack said. "I'm just tired."

"I can imagine," Lily said. "You've been through a lot."

"Yeah," Zack said, "but I'm glad you're here."

"I'm so sorry," Lily said. "When I heard what happened, I realized I should have listened to you more closely the last time we talked."

Struggling to remain calm, Zack clutched the blanket close to his chest.

"I was depressed the last time we talked, but I never thought I would end up where I am now."

Lily squeezed Zack's hand, saying, "I know it can be hard to know what to do or how to feel when you're in the middle of it."

"I just couldn't figure out how to be myself without having the people I care about hate me," Zack said.

Lily looked at Zack with tears welling in her eyes so quickly that she couldn't blink them away and said, "I'm always here. You don't have to try to solve your problems by yourself. "

After sharing a hug and shedding some tears, Zack gazed over at Lily and smiled. His smile was gentle, and it softened his tired features. Zack felt grateful to have Lily by his side.

"I have a problem you can help me figure out," Zack said.

"Sure."

Zack asked, "How do I deal with people disrespecting me?"

"Everyone has to find their own way of dealing with assholes. Let me tell you what I do, and you can decide if it would work for you," Lily answered.

"Okay, let's hear it."

"As soon as I realize someone is being disrespectful, I take a deep breath. While I'm pulling the air inside my lungs, I look away. As I blow the air out, I look at the person and try to size up where they are coming from."

Zack asked, "That's it?"

Lily continued, "Oh no. It depends on who we are talking about. If it's a religious zealot, then I suspect they want to lecture me on their beliefs. If, after I tell them that I'm not interested in discussing religion with them, they become disrespectful or aggressive, I excuse myself and walk away from the conversation."

"Doesn't it make you mad when people try to tell you how to live your life, especially when they don't know what they're talking about?"

"Of course, it makes me mad," Lily said. "Let's look at the people telling me I would be happier if I weren't a lesbian. For those people, I often ask them, 'How are things working out for you?' If they say, 'My life is great,' I smile at their confusion and say, 'I'm happy for you,' because everyone we meet is going through something in their lives, even them."

"I see what you're saying," Zack said.

"It's that I don't want to stoop to the level where I am trying to hurt someone just because they are trying to hurt me. You know, try to be cool by pushing out the positive vibes."

Laughing at Lily's cool vibe reference, Zack felt some of his troubles melting away.

Zack smiled at Lily and said, "That's a good way to look at it."

"Forget the negative people and focus on the positive people," Lily said. "I will introduce you to people whose integrity is greater than any rule book. And no, even before you ask, they are not all gay or lesbian. Some straight people will have your back, and some religious people will support you. But for sure, all good people will care about you."

Feeling relieved, knowing that different people would accept him, Zack said, "I would have never known that until you told me."

Lily grabbed Zack's hands, looked him in the eye, and said, "Don't you see, Zack? It is important to talk to people when you have a problem. They might give you a brand new perspective on what's happening in your life."

"I understand it now," Zack said. "If I feel like I am lost again, then I need to talk to someone. Someone I trust, like you."

Later that day, as Trevor walked through the automatic glass doors, he felt like he was in a dream, watching himself enter the hospital. Or maybe it wasn't even him going in the door; perhaps it was someone else.

Walking down the hospital corridors toward Zack's room, Trevor felt guilty for being so naïve and not paying enough attention to the things happening in Zack's life.

Trevor thought, *If I had done things differently, then maybe Zack wouldn't be lying in a hospital bed.*

When Trevor got to Zack's ward, it was dinner time. Zack was sitting at a table alone in the dining area, looking down at his uneaten plate of food with tears in his eyes. He had pushed the mashed potatoes and the meatloaf around so many times that by looking at his plate, you had no idea what he was eating.

Trevor hesitated for a moment when he saw Zack. Trevor thought, *What if Zack doesn't want to talk, or if I say the wrong thing?* Either way, he had to try.

Trevor walked over to Zack's table and nervously asked, "How are you doing today?"

Zack hadn't noticed Trevor's approach until he stood directly in front of him. Zack looked up at Trevor, his expression blank. He didn't say anything.

Trevor felt awkward and unsure of what to do. So he looked at his brother and smiled.

Finally, Zack said, "Please don't judge me by my worst day."

Trevor was overwhelmed with emotion. He wanted to grab his brother and run out of the hospital. He knew he couldn't do that, so he sat down at the table with Zack.

Trevor gathered his thoughts and said, "Your life is so much more than just one day."

"I know people are going to talk," Zack said.

Trevor explained, "I love you. Nobody gets to disrespect you or to try to make you explain anything."

"I am so glad that you are here," Zack said.

Overcome with emotion, Trevor began to ramble, "People bullied you, but not anymore. I will do anything to make this better for you. Just tell me what you need."

"All I can think about is how Dad is going to freak out," Zack said. "He'll never understand how alone I felt facing the fact that I'm gay."

"We both know Dad's views about homosexuality, but you are your own person," Trevor explained. "You have the right to live your life the way you want. Even if Dad never changes his mind about gay people, you deserve to be happy."

"For the first time, I feel confident that things will work out," Zack said.

Trevor and Zack hugged each other when it was time for Trevor to leave. It was a new beginning for them, but the one thing that hadn't changed was that they both knew how much the other one meant to them.

GIVE AND TAKE

Mary sat in the salon chair, looking around while her hair was being blown dry. All the other women in the salon were talking and laughing. They seemed so carefree, and Mary felt a pang of envy. She wished she could be like them, but her mind kept circling back to her daughter, Katie.

The first sign that things had begun to change was when telephone calls from Katie's friends became nonexistent, whereas before, Mary had to tell Katie to get off the phone so she could do her homework.

Shortly after the calls from her friends stopped, Katie started wanting to stay in her room. She had always been a social butterfly, always up for anything, but now she seemed to want to be alone all the time.

Mary asked her daughter if something had happened, but Katie insisted everything was fine. Mary wanted to believe Katie, but at the same time, she wondered if Katie didn't feel comfortable sharing her thoughts and feelings because she didn't want to worry her.

Mary talked to some other moms in Katie's class to see if they were experiencing the same thing with their daughters. Most of the moms said that everything was a challenge since their teenagers started going through puberty, but a few moms mentioned that Katie would often argue with the other girls and try to get her way.

Mary listened to the other moms when they talked about Katie being argumentative but decided the conflict between the girls was because Katie was trying to figure out who she was and where she fit in the world. Mary remembered her teenage years as a time of great change and transition where it was hard at times for her to find her footing.

The following Monday, Katie came home from school and announced that now that she was in the 9th grade, she didn't want to help at the animal shelter anymore.

When Mary asked if everything was okay at school, Katie replied, "School doesn't have anything to do with me working at the animal shelter. So why are you asking me stupid questions?"

Katie's snappy tone made Mary mad, so rather than having a conversation about Katie's response, Mary punished her by taking away her phone for two weeks. Mary expected Katie to return to her old self as soon as she realized there were consequences for her actions.

Even before Katie had gotten her phone back, her teacher, Ms. Johnson, requested a parent-teacher conference. Katie wasn't turning in homework assignments and was having trouble not interrupting while Ms. Johnson gave instructions in the classroom. There were also complaints from several of the girls in the class that Katie was bossy.

Katie became very defensive when Mary talked to her about what her teacher had said.

"Ms. Johnson picks on me and only says those things because she never has time to answer my questions," Katie said. "So I have a problem with her, not the girls in my class."

Ms. Johnson had been Mark's, Katie's brother's, teacher three years ago. Mark liked Ms. Johnson, and Mary appreciated how she kept up with all the students in her classroom. So, the difference between how Ms. Johnson and Katie saw things let Mary know something was happening. But what?

Mary thought a get-together at the house would be a good way for her to gain some insight into any conflicts Katie might be having with her friends. Katie was hesitant at first, but Mary eventually convinced her to have a party by offering to come up with a list of words and phrases for the charade game.

On the day of the get-together, only seven girls showed up, although Katie had passed out seventeen invitations. With eight girls, counting Katie, the girls were divided into two teams with four players on each team.

On each turn, the previous person acting out the charade would pick someone on their team to act out what was on the next card. When it came time for Katie to determine the next person to be the actor, she held out the new card to the girl she was pretending to choose and then pulled it back, hiding it behind her back. After Katie repeatedly did this to all the girls on her team, they insisted that Katie hurry up and choose someone. After several minutes of Katie's teasing, the girls ignored her and picked their team's new actor.

Katie was infuriated when the girls on her team didn't wait for her to pick the next actor. She grabbed the deck of cards and threw them all over the floor.

Mary was sitting in a living room chair, observing Katie as she teased the other girls. She was unsure whether to intervene immediately or wait for a private chat with Katie about her annoying behavior. But, when Katie threw the cards, she stood up and firmly told her, "Katie, you need to pick up the cards."

Katie glared at her mom, walked over to the dining room table, and sat slumped down in a chair with her arms folded.

Noticing the other girls nervously fidgeting with their clothes and avoiding eye contact with anyone, Mary could see the party was quickly becoming a disaster. She attempted to distract Katie from her lousy mood by asking her to help carry some sodas from the refrigerator. Katie responded to her mother's request by staring at her and tapping her finger on the dining room table.

The tension in the room made the girls feel uneasy. They grabbed their cell phones and texted their parents. The party was over, and they were ready to go home.

When the girls' parents arrived, Mary tried to coax Katie to come to the front door and say goodbye to her friends, but Katie wouldn't budge from the dining room chair. Katie didn't seem to care if she lost her friends or not.

Mark, a senior in high school, had avoided all the confusion at his sister's party with the excuse that he had a study group at the library. Mark had an A in the class but had no desire to be around a bunch of ninth-grade girls. Instead, he was interested in girls his age, like Liz.

At the library, Liz brought up Katie.

"I'm sure you know my brother is in your sister's class at school. Last night at the dinner table, he told us a story about how Katie had been sent to the principal's office twice in one week for interrupting the teacher."

"Okay," Mark said. "So, Katie interrupted the teacher."

Liz continued, "So my mom asked me if you ever acted like that or got into trouble at school. I told her no, of course not."

"What else did she say?" Mark asked.

"She said that if your mom made Katie listen, she wouldn't be so rude," Liz answered.

After the study group broke up, Mark went home to talk to his mom about everything Liz had told him. Mary responded by saying that she was frustrated with how Katie acted, and sometimes, she questioned if her parenting was to blame for Katie's rebellious behavior.

Mary also talked to her husband, Steve, about Katie's behavior. Steve listened patiently, but he hadn't noticed any changes. However, he did become concerned after learning about Katie's actions at the party.

Before she could help Katie, Mary knew that she needed to learn more about Katie's school day and get a better sense of Katie's interactions with her teachers and classmates. So Mary contacted the school and started volunteering in the library on Wednesdays.

On her third Wednesday volunteering, Mary bit into a hard piece of candy and chipped her tooth. Her dentist was able to fit her in that day, but the appointment was for the same time school would let out. Mary called several of the moms from Katie's class to ask if Katie could come over to their house for an hour after school, but everyone she called made excuses about having appointments after school themselves.

Mary asked Evelyn, another mom from Katie's class who volunteered in the school's front office, if Katie could come over to her house after school while she went to the dentist. Evelyn told Mary it would be best if Katie came over when she had a parent with her because Katie was hard to handle when she got upset.

Mary was disappointed about the other moms being too busy for Katie to come over, but Evelyn's offhanded remarks stung Mary the most. Mary was concerned that she might be overlooking something about Katie's school life, so she decided to talk to Ms. Johnson the next day.

Mary woke up early the following day, feeling anxious about talking to Ms. Johnson. She had been worried about Katie's behavior at home for a while now, and Katie's behavior at school, which Ms. Johnson had addressed at the last parent-teacher conference, might be getting worse.

Mary showed up at the school half an hour before the first students were due to arrive. She went to Katie's classroom and peered through the open door. Seeing that Ms. Johnson was busy working on some papers at her desk, Mary knocked on the door to get her attention.

Ms. Johnson stood up from behind her desk when she saw Mary and invited her into the classroom. She smiled and asked, "What can I do. for you?"

Mary took a deep breath. "I'm here to talk about my daughter," she said.

"I'm so glad you came in," said Ms. Johnson. "I've been meaning to talk to you about Katie."

Mary told Ms. Johnson about some of the things that Katie had been doing at home, like wanting to stay in her room, being rude at the party, and talking back.

Ms. Johnson listened carefully. When Mary finished, she said, "Katie has been talking back at school too and disrupting the classroom. Katie is a bright girl, but for some reason, she isn't meeting her full potential. Perhaps if Katie met with the school psychologist, he could help her become more successful academically and socially."

The recommendation for Katie to seek professional help was tough for Mary to hear. Her knee-jerk reaction was that Katie was immature but would grow out of it. At other times, her thoughts would flip-flop between denying that Katie needed help and realizing that Katie was struggling. After a week of thoughtful consideration, Mary agreed to let Katie see the school psychologist after the upcoming winter break.

Mary woke up on the first day of winter break feeling relieved that Katie would have two weeks off from school. She had noticed that Katie became withdrawn after coming home from school, only giving short, one-word answers to questions. Lately, Katie had also been getting easily frustrated at home over minor things—she started crying when she couldn't find a blue marker and threw a magazine at her brother for changing the TV channel. Mary hoped the break would help Katie relax and feel comfortable enough to open up about what had caused her to feel so stressed in the first place.

Mary attempted to initiate a conversation with Katie by expressing her willingness to listen to her and support her, but Katie seemed hesitant to talk about the issue that was troubling her. Katie would only say that her emotions made her feel like she was riding a seesaw. When the seesaw was up, she felt like she could manage, but when it went down, she was terrified.

One afternoon, Mary and Katie went grocery shopping together. On their way home, Katie decided to open up to her mom a little bit to see how she would react.

"Can I tell you a secret?" Katie asked.

"You can tell me anything," Mary answered.

Katie disclosed, "One of the guys that worked at the animal shelter tried to hurt me."

"What do you mean tried to hurt you?" Mary asked.

"Why are you asking me all these questions? I feel like you don't believe me," Katie said.

"I'm sorry. I'm here to listen, not to ask you a bunch of questions," Mary answered.

Filled with self-blame about the entire ordeal, Katie blurted out, "I should have never gone in the storage room. He held me up against the wall the first time and tried to pull down my pants. I kicked him in his shinbone and ran away. He tried to pull me into the storage room twice after that. I told him I would scream, so he let me go."

"I understand now why you quit helping at the animal shelter. I really need you to tell me who he is."

"He said that it was all my fault. He knew that I wanted his attention by the clothes I wore," Katie said.

"This is all his fault. Just tell me who he is, and I'll make sure he never hurts anyone again."

When Mary got home, she discussed what Katie had told her with Steve, and he insisted they call the police. When the police arrived, they saw Katie sitting in a chair, crying. They took their time taking Katie's statement, letting her take breaks whenever needed. When the police began collecting personal identification information from Katie's parents, she suddenly claimed that she was feeling unwell. She said that she was going to lie down in her room.

After the police left, Mary went up to Katie's room. Mary's heart ached as she stepped into Katie's room. The sight of her daughter crying with her face buried in her hands made Mary wish that she could take away the pain that made Katie cry like this, but at the same time, Mary was struggling with her anger over Katie's loss of innocence. She was angry that she couldn't confront the person who caused Katie's pain and even blamed herself for not protecting Katie.

Ultimately, her love for her daughter won over her simmering rage. Wanting to prioritize comfort and understanding for her daughter, Mary told Katie there was someone who could help. The school psychologist was kind and understanding. He could help her navigate these feelings, this... unfair thing that should have never happened.

Katie was hesitant about her mother's suggestion, but after her mother assured her that she wouldn't have to discuss anything she was uncomfortable with, Katie agreed. The only condition was that her mother kept her secret about what happened in the storage room from her teacher and friends.

Katie found the psychologist easy to talk to and non-judgmental, allowing her to open up about what happened. When Katie expressed guilt about the incident, the school psychologist knew he had to dispel Katie's self-blame in response to the trauma.

The school psychologist explained, "Some girls are afraid of reporting a boy's bad behavior to an adult because they worry someone might blame them. But it's not the girl's responsibility to control or fix a dangerous boy's behavior. Boys are solely responsible for their own actions."

"He made me believe it was my fault," Katie said.

"When that boy tried to make you feel responsible for his bad behavior because of the clothes you were wearing, he was wrong," the school psychologist explained. "He's responsible for the choices he made, not you."

After meeting with Katie several times, the school psychologist determined that Katie was anxious that something similar to her experience in the storage room would happen again. She tried to prevent this by controlling things in her life, but when she realized she couldn't control everything, she lashed out and became aggressive at home and school.

Two months after Katie started therapy, she felt safe again. Her mood and her behavior began to improve dramatically. Her grades were high B's, and her teacher commented that she was a pleasure to have in class.

Mary was very proud of Katie's resilience, but at the same time, she felt the need to protect her daughter. Realizing how much time Katie spent at school, Mary added another afternoon to her volunteering schedule as a way to stay more involved in Katie's life.

The other volunteers at school would chit-chat with Mary about recipes and fundraising for the school, but when it came to the subject of Katie, Mary found three types of reactions from the other moms. Katie was a taboo subject; they were surprised at how friendly Katie was, or they hoped all the chaos was under control.

The sly mumble about the chaos not returning stuck out the most in Mary's mind. She wanted to scream that none of this was Katie's fault, but it was Katie's secret to tell.

Cecelia was a new mom at the school who volunteered in the library on the same day as Mary. Her family had recently relocated to the area after her husband started a new job.

Cecilia was using the copy machine in the teacher's lounge one afternoon when she overheard a group of moms discussing Katie's behavior. They commented that it was only a matter of time before she started acting like a brat again because her mom didn't discipline her. The negativity and judgmental attitudes of these moms made Cecilia feel very uncomfortable. She was interested in building relationships, not in trying to divide people.

Cecilia felt compelled to reach out to Mary. She wanted to talk to her away from the ears of the school gossipers, so she invited Mary to a local coffee shop.

The next day, Cecilia and Mary met at the coffee shop, where they both ordered the house blend. As soon as they were handed their drinks, they found a table.

"This is good," Cecilia said. "I've never had the house blend before."

"Me neither," Mary said. "But it's really good."

They sat in silence for a moment, enjoying their coffee.

"You remind me of a good friend I met in college," Cecilia said. "Her name is Natalie. She volunteered in the library while we were in college. She's one of my closest friends now."

"When was the last time you saw her?"

"After college, she moved to a different state, so now we mostly keep up with each other through texting and video calls. I haven't seen her in person for over a year and a half."

"You must miss her," Mary replied.

"I do," Cecelia said. "She's married and has two children. One of her children was recently diagnosed with autism."

"How did she take the news?" Mary asked.

"She became very anxious about her son's future."

Mary took a deep breath and said, "I'm sure you have heard through the grapevine that my daughter has had some problems, and she was seeing the school psychologist."

"I was disappointed that some parents have no problem gossiping or speculating about other people. It made me uncomfortable because I knew if they gossiped to me, then the chances were that they would gossip about me. I don't trust a gossiper."

"Some people don't understand how hurtful words can be," Mary said. "It was hard enough for me to deal with Katie's struggles, much less having to deal with the other parents being critical of Katie and me."

Cecelia gave Mary a reassuring smile and said, "I can only imagine how many different feelings are involved. Natalie told me that after her son's diagnosis, some parents would avoid her, even turn and go the other way when they saw her coming. Their reactions made her believe that she was a terrible mother and made her question what else she had done wrong."

"I know exactly how she must have felt," Mary said.

Cecelia took a sip of her coffee. "After listening to all the gossipers at school, I'm sure you could."

"It's refreshing to talk to someone who doesn't just want to know what's going on but actually cares. You are an amazing person," Mary said.

Wanting to let Mary know that she understood some of the challenges when dealing with people, Cecelia said, "Some people don't realize that no one would choose to have problems with their mental health any more than they would choose to have cancer."

Feeling understood for the first time in such a long time, Mary said, "It can be very frustrating when people are quick to judge a person when they don't have any idea what's happening in their life."

"Some people don't know a lot about mental health, so they quickly jump to a conclusion about what it means to be mentally healthy or unhealthy."

Mary agreed, "One of the other parents at school blamed me for Katie's struggles. It was all my fault for not being strict enough."

Cecelia shook her head in disgust and said, "Wouldn't it be wonderful if people were more understanding and less judgmental."

"Thank you for inviting me for coffee," Mary said. "I enjoy talking with you."

Cecelia said. "Of course. Somehow, I knew that I would enjoy talking with you too."

Mary knew that the best way to gain a friend was to be one, so she invited Cecelia for lunch later that week.

THANK YOU

Thank you for purchasing a copy of my book.

Please consider leaving a review for *Blooming Through The Cracks: Inspiring Stories of Resilience* on Amazon and Goodreads.

I look forward to sharing more stories with you soon.

Thank you,
Sandra Damiani

ABOUT THE AUTHOR

Sandra spends her time at the intersection of writing and advocating for children in the juvenile court system. Her work with abused and neglected children and experiences with different life events inspired her to begin her writing journey in 2022.

Sandra's foremost reason for writing is to use the protagonists' experiences in her stories to help her readers understand and empathize with others. Sandra hopes that when people contemplate other people's perspectives and accept that their experiences are not the only lived experiences, they move closer to understanding that we are all in this together.

Sandra is an honorably retired Air Force veteran. Her military career took her from California to Washington, DC, seven European countries, and the Middle East. As a result, different cultures and worldviews are fascinating to her.

When Sandra isn't writing, you can find her reading, driving with the music blaring, traveling, hiking, or floating in a kayak, contemplating her purpose in life.

You can find out what Sandra is working on next at:

www.sandradamianiauthor.com

https://www.instagram.com/sandra.damiani.writer/